1984

Steve Turner, an associate professor of sociology at the University of South Florida, is a member of Creative Interchange Consultants and has conducted workshops on conflict management for managers in government, industry, business, and health sectors.

Frank Weed is a professor of sociology at the University of Texas and has written many articles on the subject of complex organizations.

A SPECTRUM BOOK

Prentice-Hall, Inc., Englewood Cliffs, New Jersey 07632

STEVE TURNER
FRANK WEED

Practical Solutions
Any Manager Can Use

CONFLICT
IN
ORGANIZATIONS

Library of Congress Cataloging in Publication Data

Turner, Steve
   Conflict in organizations.

   "A Spectrum Book"
   Bibliography: p.
   Includes index.
   1. Conflict management.   I. Weed, Frank
II. Title.
HD42.T87   1983   658.3'145   82-22967
ISBN 0-13-167395-5
ISBN 0-13-167387-4 (pbk.)

This book is available at a special discount when ordered
in bulk quantities. Contact Prentice-Hall, Inc., General
Publishing Division, Special Sales, Englewood Cliffs, N.J. 07632

ISBN 0-13-167395-5

ISBN 0-13-167387-4 {PBK.}

A SPECTRUM BOOK Printed in the United States of America

1 2 3 4 5 6 7 8 9 10

Editorial/production supervision by Alberta Boddy
Cover design © 1983 by Jeannette Jacobs
Manufacturing buyer: Cathie Lenard

Prentice-Hall International, Inc., *London*
Prentice-Hall of Australia Pty., Limited, *Sydney*
Prentice-Hall of Canada, Ltd., *Toronto*
Prentice-Hall of India Private, Limited, *New Delhi*
Prentice-Hall of Japan, Inc., *Tokyo*
Prentice-Hall of Southeast Asia Pte., Ltd., *Singapore*
Whitehall Books, Limited, *Wellington, New Zealand*
Editora Prentice-Hall do Brasil Ltda., *Rio de Janeiro*

To Summer, young Summer,
Michelle, Pat, Tracy, and Sarah

CONTENTS

PREFACE

This book shows you how to effectively think through problems of organizational conflict, gives you guidelines for action, and points out some of the pitfalls and problems that various solutions might create. It teaches you the basic concepts you will need to think through alternative solutions, and it illustrates these concepts by examining everyday examples drawn from many sectors—from industry, offices, government, as well as from education, hospitals, and other service industries—and from many levels—from waiters to a chief executive officer of a large international corporation. You will learn concepts that apply to all these situations. Without immersing you in a cold sea of jargon, this book gives you practical, usable ideas expressed in an informal and direct way.

Almost everyone who has worked at a supervisory level has been exposed to some management training, which has often been training that has emphasized psychological gimmicks. Problems of conflict rarely respond to gimmicks. This book stresses the *situational* causes of conflict. The solutions that the book considers are things that any manager can do, such as making changes in work routines, assignments, or structure, or making informal arrangements. The book teaches you how to recognize the features of work arrangements that produce conflict and how to watch out for "solutions" that produce new conflicts.

Organizational conflict is a double drain on the quality of life. For the participants in conflict situations it is a drain on the quality of their work life, their self-esteem, and their health. For the rest of us it is also a drain because conflict—whether overt or concealed—is a major source of productivity problems, which means that it is a cause of excessive costs of goods and services.

The conflict discussed in this book is not "conflict" in the sense of positive struggle between opposing interests and ideas that results in new and better agreements, new and stronger solidarity, and renewed trust. The sort of conflict dealt with in this book is the kind that hurts—everyday grinding resentment and irritation, distrust, personal bad feelings, as well as open displays of anger. Most organizations have some hurtful conflict, more or less concealed, all the time, at least some place in the organization. So this book is not about an aberrant phenomenon: it is about a common fact of organizational life.

The everyday ways in which people talk and think about the people in conflict situations and the ways in which people react to conflict often obscure the problems, making them even more frustrating. Most conflict situations result from pressures and stresses involving conflicting demands, insufficient or inappropriate power to act, or threats to a person's self-esteem. These problems, once recognized, can be solved by changing work arrangements. However, there are pitfalls to such changes. These pitfalls must be understood so that they can be avoided.

The lesson of this book is that organizational conflict can be dealt with. As with any managerial problem, it requires proper thinking through, and how to think it through can be learned. Armed with the basic tools that this book provides and guided by its ideas and examples, you will be ready to tackle your organizational conflict problems and will be able to follow through with a workable solution.

Many people have contributed to this book, in various ways. Summer Turner labored over the text and made it readable. Khaleah Bryant and Kathy Sewell typed faithfully and competently under trying circumstances. Finally, our students in conflict management training sessions and our consultees have provided elements of many of the examples discussed in the book. The examples have been altered for ease of exposition; none of them are intended to characterize specific actual persons or organizations.

CONFLICT!

Conflict! Clear images—the angry worker or manager, a shouting match, a nerve-shattering confrontation—come to mind when we think of conflict in organizations. Yet overt conflict, where it does occur, is usually only the tip of an iceberg of submerged conflict. Often no overt confrontation occurs, even when there are serious conflicts, when many people in the situation have feelings of anger, hurt, frustration, and a sense that they are being handled, used, and otherwise dealt with in bad faith.

In this chapter, we discuss the reasons for the submerged nature of most conflict. The chapter is divided into three parts. In the first part we deal with the problem of individual responses to conflict, particularly some characteristic response styles. By response styles we mean the types of feeling-responses people have when faced with conflict. In the next part we take up the tactics that people use in conflict situations—tactics that are the source of trouble for the organization. In the third part we talk about communication and especially about the common notion that if people could just communicate, organizational conflicts would vanish.

RESPONSE STYLES

People involved in the field of management training and organizational development training have a few tricks of the trade for making people aware of how they respond to conflict and how others respond. One of these gimmicks works like this. The people in the training group are asked to close their eyes. Then they are asked to think of someone in the organization or in their lives with whom they feel in conflict. The trainer then asks them to imagine that they are walking in a shopping center, when suddenly they recognize this person in the distance. The person comes closer. "How," the trainer asks, "do you feel inside?" "Finally the person arrives," the trainer says. "What do you do?"

One point of the exercise is to show that not everyone in a group responds in the same way. Yet people, whether men or women, or experienced administrators or people who are first-time supervisors, describe responses that fall into a relatively narrow range: They say different things, but not many different kinds of things. Here are some examples:

1. I would tighten up inside. Then I'd smile and say, "Hello," and get it over with.
2. The feeling would be something like "you've got your nerve." Then I'd let the situation take over, and respond to whatever she did.
3. Punch him out [said laughingly].
4. Be civil, pretend it's a normal situation with a normal person, and make it brief.
5. Say dirty words about her—to myself!
6. Become absorbed with something else.
7. Pretend there had been no conflict.
8. Inside, I would be wondering how he felt, and whether he was still upset or angry. Then I would smile and nod.

9. I would try to "smooth the water" and say something that showed that I wanted to resolve our problems.
10. Tell him off.
11. Just ignore her.
12. I'd try to face the issues with him. I would use the meeting as a chance to discuss our problems, or at least to set up a time at work when we could talk about things.

The trainer has purposely set up a difficult situation in the minds of his subjects, trying to produce their most characteristic reaction, based on their feelings about this kind of personal encounter. The list gives a good idea of the gut responses people have in conflict situations.

The obvious point to be made about these lists of responses— the thing that leaps from the page and impresses the group—is that few of these responses get us closer to any resolution of the problems. Most of them *avoid* the issue or conceal it.

One might classify responses in various ways. A useful list of types of reactions might be:

Addressers
  1. First steppers
  2. Confronters
Concealers
  1. Feeling-swallowers
  2. Subject-changers
  3. Avoiders, quitters
Attackers
  1. Up-front attackers
  2. Behind-the-back attackers

Addressers

Addressers are rare birds. They are the people who see a conflict in a particular way—that is, have a unique view of the conflict—and try to resolve it by getting their opponent to agree with them on something. They are willing to take the risk of being the first to act to deal with the problem. First steppers are people who will offer to make a gesture of friendliness, agreeableness, or sympathy with the other person's situation, or just to acknowledge the dispute in exchange for something similar in return. They feel that some trust has to be established first, before anyone can get down to business, and that this takes a gesture in response. We might call this a form of face-saving ritual, because it provides a means of extricating the person from the encounter if the gesture is not returned. The first stepper is testing the water.

The confronter takes the plunge. When a person confronts, the act of confrontation becomes a fact, something that can be referred to later, and it changes the relation just by having happened. Confronters think they have enough of an atmosphere of trust to make the issue public, either because they are in authority and have the more secure position, or because they feel that things are so bad that they have nothing to lose by a confrontation. In both cases, it's a matter of risk. Confrontation always means risk; some people will think they can afford the risk, and some people will not.

Concealers

Concealers can't or won't take the risk of saying something. Feeling-swallowers are concealers who swallow their feelings and smile, even though they have definite feelings about being wronged or put-upon. They don't do anything about the situation, at least in the presence of anyone at the workplace, in spite of the fact that the work situation is the source of enormous pain and unhappiness. If you think about the many ways people blow off steam or share their troubles, you can see how much emotion the feeling-swallower is swallowing. When you go to the water cooler and complain about the boss, the salespeople, or the dietician, you are sharing your troubles with your co-workers. They commiserate, and you feel better. The feeling-swallower doesn't get to feel better. Indeed, often the feelings of anger, once swallowed, become feelings of self-doubt or self-hatred for putting up with an intolerable situation.

Feeling-swallowers can be hard to spot. Some people will get their feelings out in some contexts, such as with a few trusted friends, yet they may keep their feelings bottled up in the presence of superiors or with people they do not trust. The true feeling-swallower type treats other people as if they were overbearing, or as if they were people whose approval is so important that it is dangerous to risk offending them by showing true feelings.

Subject-changers can be even harder to spot. The real issues are too hot for the subject-changers to handle, so they find a topic on which they can agree with the people with whom they feel in conflict. This is a fine mechanism for avoiding the unpleasantness of an out-in-the-open disagreement, but it creates problems both for the people who use it and for the organization of which they are a part. The things that need to be changed to solve the conflict may not be the things on which an agreement is easy to reach. For example, one frequently finds that splashy efforts at trying to reach a consensus on goals, such as Management by Objectives meetings, turn out to be massive exercises in conflict avoidance by subject changing. The great sense of common purpose and direction that everyone feels after these meetings quickly vanishes when the participants face the real conflicts and aggravations of daily life in the organization, just as the great feeling of going out to win that a football team has after the half-time pep talk can vanish in the face of real opponents.

Avoiders and quitters can also be hard to spot. Avoiders often go out of the way to do their job without getting into hassles. Almost everyone, of course, does this to some degree, discretion being the better part of valor. In the short run it works, from the day you walk home from school the long way to avoid the local bully, to the day when, as an adult, you write a report in a way that avoids problems with someone with whom you must work harmoniously every day in order to get your own work done. There is still usually a cost to avoiding, of course, but patience frequently serves in a world where things are always changing. Bullies move away or find other people to pick on, and troublesome people get transferred or change jobs; thus, some problems do take care of themselves.

Quitting is a way out when patience fails, and the prospect of quitting is a good prop for patience. Most people can put up with unpleasantness if they can see some end to it. But quitters and avoiders rarely tell the truth about *why* they are quitting or why they take the long way home. There are always other "good" reasons that can be given for doing almost anything, and these will be the reasons that are given. Sometimes these explanations will be elaborately developed. Sometimes the people who give the reasons will believe them themselves.

Attackers

Attackers give reasons for their actions, too—usually self-serving reasons—and believe them as well. Unlike feeling-swallowers, who can't let their feelings out, attackers can't keep their feelings in. People who are angry usually find a target for their anger, often choosing the wrong targets or getting angry at someone for things that aren't really anyone's "fault." It's usually easier to put up with people like this by agreeing with them rather than risk getting on their bad side, so people like this get a lot of positive feedback from their peers. The anger that they feel seems justified by the positive feedback, even if the people who are agreeing with them think the anger is misplaced or even a bit crazy. Such angry people can turn even the most lukewarm response into "support" for their side of an issue.

Angry people who get their feelings out in the open—up-front attackers—make work more pleasant for the person who is the target, because that person can get some positive feedback—sympathy, support, and agreement—as well. Angry people who engage in behind-the-back tactics, such as bad mouthing and gossip, are harder to handle, because the target, the person criticized, is never quite sure what the actual criticisms are, and of course, can't be sure about what people really believe.

The lesson of this list of characteristic response styles is that people deal with conflicts in ways that often obscure the problems. Indeed, most responses conceal the problems in one way or another. However, just because the problems are concealed doesn't mean that there are no consequences for the organization. The fact that most people respond in ways that conceal the problems leads to a standard management mistake in dealing with conflict situations. Because the visible people in the conflict situation are the attackers and con-fronters, the temptation is for the manager to think that these people *are* the problem. The manager gets into the habit of dealing with problems by asking "who?" when the right questions are "what?" and "why?" If there are "problem people" in a conflict situation, they are usually, as we said earlier, just the tip of an iceberg of un-happy people who respond differently to problems. These people, as we will see in the next section and throughout the book, have ways of dealing with their situation that are usually more damaging to the organization than are "attacking" and "confronting." Now we will talk about some of these tactics for dealing with conflict.

TACTICS

Blocks and Covers

To protect themselves against hassles and anger, people in organiza-tions use various "blocking" and "covering" tactics. These tactics are also part of the story in conflict situations. The relation between response styles and choice of tactics is this: Although some people tend to prefer some tactics more than others, the range of responses used by any given person is likely to be broader than the person's characteristic response styles. Thus, few people respond in all of the styles listed here, while many people use the full range of blocking and covering tactics, as the situation demands.

Ask yourself this question. "Who determines my salary level and, in particular, my merit raises and bonuses?" Unless you are in a bureaucracy that permits almost no discretion over salaries, or unless you are in a small organization, you will be hard-pressed to give a precise answer to this question. On an issue that is this important to people and which is such a frequent cause of anger and resentment, it is a standard tactic to *obscure authority* or to make it ambiguous, so that it is never precisely clear who is to blame for a particular decision.

This tactic can be exploited in various ways. In Stanley Milgram's famous study of authority, the experimental subjects were asked to press buttons that they thought would produce a painful electric shock in another person. When a subject objected, he or she was told something like this: "The experiment requires that you follow directions." The "experiment" becomes like a person; thus, the authority of the experimenter becomes obscured.

Of course, blocking and obscuring tactics aren't just used by people in authority. Underlings as well as bosses frequently hide behind established practices. A standard army tactic is contained in this advice: "When someone asks why you are doing something this way, just say, 'that's how it was done when I got here.'" Rules can be good "blocks," too. Many rules can be interpreted in such a way that blame can be shifted to the rule. Nowadays it is common to blame the possibility of a lawsuit for inability to perform a practice or action. "If we did that and something went wrong, we could be sued."

Committees

The practice of setting up a committee serves to make authority ambiguous. The good effect of this is that it allows people to do the right thing without taking personal responsibility—and criticism and abuse—for the decision. After all, members of a committee can blame the other members for the outcome, even when it has been the outcome they each desired or thought was right. This fact of diminished responsibility cuts both ways. People can do the *wrong* thing under the cover of a committee process, such as pursue their personal interests and vendettas. And since no "Monday-morning quarterback" can ever really sort out the whys and wherefores of a committee decision, no one can actually make the blame stick.

Managers and administrators sometimes use committees to hide behind. In one university, the president, who later went on to become president of one of the most important universities in the United States, used committees as a technique for dealing with every decision likely to produce conflict. He would appoint a committee, which would conduct a detailed investigation and send him a long report. He would then thank the committee profusely for its hard work. Then he would read the report. If it didn't say what he wanted it to say, he would wait a year, and, with much fanfare, appoint *another* committee, with a similar assignment, as though the first committee never existed. When this committee produced a report, he would do the same thing. On one occasion he had to go through *three* committees before one produced the result he wanted. Then, he "accepted" their recommendation as though he were graciously submitting to it. If someone complained about the decision, he would point out that "this was the recommendation of a committee that studied the problem for seven months."

COMMUNICATION

How Addressing Fails

The point of this little story is that shifting or avoiding blame—"covering your ass," or CYA, as they say —is a basic practice of organizational life. Accomplished practitioners of CYA may not be greatly admired for their job performance, but they are never blamed for anything that happens, either. CYA neutralizes opponents. Thus, the "addresser," the person who sees a problem and tries to confront it or make the first step in reconciliation, may come up against the blank wall of a blame-shifting CYA strategy.

This is our first unpleasant truth. If, after beginning this chapter by listing "conflict response styles," we had asked, "Which is the best type of person to be?" we would all say, "Be an 'addresser,' because an addresser takes responsibility and deals with problems in a positive way." It is nevertheless true that this approach rarely works. In a world of concealers and attackers, in which blame-shifting is standard practice, the response to a conscientious addresser is likely to be, "Well, it's not my fault, because that's the way it was done when I got here," or, "You lousy crumb, you've been screwing me up for all these years by not doing your work, and now you have the gall to complain to me! I bet you've been running to the vice-president with all this garbage . . . " or, "Yes, whatever you say" (and then this person goes to his friends and says, "You wouldn't believe what so-and-so told me . . . "). If an organization operates in such a way, so that nobody wants to take the responsibility for a problem, then you can bet that nobody will be willing to take responsibility for a solution, either.

Another sad truth about "addressers" is this: Even when two people with the best intentions want to work out their problems, there is no guarantee that they will manage to define their problems in such a way that they can find a solution. If things were really so simple, there would be more happy marriages! In marriages, people often articulate their dissatisfactions with ease, only to discover that, when they get what they think they want, they are still dissatisfied. This applies to organizations, as well. If people find a solution, there is no guarantee that they will be able to live up to it, or that this "solution" won't cause more problems or different problems.

When "Communication" Makes Things Worse

One solution that is often considered is "improving communication" on the assumption that conflict is always caused by misunderstanding. Although misunderstandings can cause conflict, few conflicts are simple misunderstandings that can be improved with more communication. We can begin to understand why "communication" fails just by considering the list of responses at the beginning of the chapter. We can see this more clearly if we consider a typical conflict situation and how different types of responses bear on it.

The organization we will look at is a firm that services electric motors. The production units are divided according to the size of the motors. There is one "sales" unit, which takes orders, picks up motors to be repaired, and delivers the repaired motors. The problem appears to be a morale problem. The supervisor of the small motor repair unit, a first-rate repair specialist, constantly criticizes the truck drivers for being lazy, for not doing their jobs, and for anything else he can think of. The firm is a small one: thirty-six employees, including three managers, nine drivers, and four repair units, each with one supervisor and five workers. In a small firm like this, constant criticisms and backbiting is a major problem and the one that is the most frequently encountered.

The managers face this problem as a morale problem. The one thing they want most is for the supervisor of the small motor unit to shut up. They think that he's doing a good job, in fact a superb job. If they didn't think this, they would have fired him long ago. The drivers get along well with all the other units, and the managers think they do a good job.

The small motor supervisor is an "attacker"—though he might think of himself as an addresser. He thinks he knows what the problem is, and says something about it. He thinks that if the company hired some good drivers that could do their job correctly, then everything would be better. This is a typical approach to such a problem, and it's based on the "good personnel" theory of organizational harmony, which asks "who?" not "why?" and therefore almost never gets to the source of the problem. The repair supervisor is not a psychologist or human relations expert, so he doesn't think about the problem in any fancy way. He just tells it like he sees it.

The effect of "communication" in this situation is to make things worse. The drivers get mad when they hear the criticisms. They feel the criticisms are outlandish and that there's nothing they can do about them, so the supervisor seems like a jerk to them. They begin to suspect that maybe he is screwing them up by not having jobs completed when they've promised them to customers.

In this situation the drivers were avoiders. They pretended there wasn't a problem and tried to be nice, or at least civil, because to get their job done they needed the repair work to be done in a predictable, timely way. They were furious about the unfair criticism, but they didn't want an open fight, because they could not see any satisfactory solution. Nothing would make the small motor supervisor stop feeling as he did, even if some manager did make him shut up. Shutting him up would not change his feelings toward the drivers, and he could find other ways of showing his discontent, which could be even more disruptive.

The Situational Explanation

The identification of the real, underlying problem in the motor repair unit goes beyond "improving communication" between the
small motor supervisor and the drivers. If we ask the simple question,
*How does the work relationship between the small motor supervisor
and the other parts of the company, including the drivers, cause the
supervisor to have these negative feelings?* we might get closer to the
real problem.

First we observe that the four repair units competed with each
other, and that this competition was, to some extent, a healthy thing,
because it kept all the workers on their toes. The managers didn't
really encourage competition, but they didn't discourage it, either.
The supervisors tended, rightly or wrongly, to think that they were
being compared to one another, but when we look at their shops, we
see that they faced slightly different problems.

For the larger motor shops, the problems were mostly internal.
It took a long time to repair a big motor, and the speed or smooth-
ness of the job depended primarily on how things went within the
shop. Thus, the supervisor and his workers had control over most of
the uncertainties in the process.

The small motor shop did much the same work, but the jobs
were smaller; so the primary source of the disturbance in the work
flow was the *pace* at which the jobs came in. If the drivers didn't
pick up many small motors, the shop would be idle, and this would
make the shop, and the supervisor, look bad. If they picked up a lot
of motors, and the customers expected them back quickly, it made
the shop look bad, too, because they couldn't get the work done on
time.

In either case the small motor supervisor felt that the drivers
were responsible for making his division look bad when compared to
the operations of the larger motor shops. The supervisor felt he was
being pushed around by delivery truck drivers who couldn't care less
about his problems of scheduling the repair work, so he reacted by
finding fault with everything they did.

We bring up this example to illustrate one of the basic points in
understanding conflict in organizations. Stated simply, the point of
conflict is not always the center of the problem. Later, we will elaborate this idea. For now, just note, first, that the supervisor's feelings

were caused by the competitive spirit that had developed between the supervisors of the four repair units and second, that the combination of the competitive spirit and the uneven work load in the small motor unit caused a great deal of frustration, which was focused on the most apparent cause, the drivers. If we just brought the supervisor and the drivers together in an effort to improve communication, they would have defended themselves by insisting that they were doing their jobs; in fact, they all were.

Who's in Charge?

In later chapters we'll consider some solutions to the problems facing the motor repair firm. For now, let's consider one more aspect of the motor repair unit example that is a recurrent source of trouble. The problem is this: Most of us are not in control of the pace of our work. The way in which other people arrange their activities produces demands on us. One way of looking at the organization is to ask, *Who depends on whom to get the job done?* A part of every organization is the system of status that defines certain people as those who give orders and control the work done by other people who take orders. The flow of communication that deals with the control of work is expected to go from the supervisor (the high status person) to the worker (the lower status person).

The expectation of who is supposed to tell whom what to do gets in the way of a free exchange of ideas and information. The person who is following the orders can respond in various ways. One way is to say nothing. Another way is to explain his or her point of view to the person giving the orders. "Talking this out," however, isn't likely to be especially productive. When status is an issue, it gets in the way of talk.

To see why this is so, let's go back to the example of the conflict between the small motor supervisor and the drivers. When a customer puts pressure on a driver to get an electric motor repaired and returned in a hurry, the driver passes the pressure on to the supervisor by saying that the customer is in a hurry for the motor. The supervisor is expected to then satisfy the customer. After all, the business is based on good, reliable service. The problem is that in this situation the supervisor (a high status person) is expected to satisfy the directive of the truck driver (a lower status person). The supervisor may resentfully ask, "Who is supposed to be in charge here, the driver or me?" When the work situation requires that a lower status person give orders to a higher status person, you can expect nothing but trouble, because one of the issues in the conflict is the status system itself.

Suppose we did not recognize these underlying problems in the organization of work in the firm that services electric motors, and instead focused on the supervisor. In this case the supervisor's type of response was as an attacker. Suppose that he had been a concealer instead. Would the company then have worked smoothly with a supervisor who expressed no frustration with the drivers? The frustration would still have been there. It might have been expressed by slowing the work pace so that everyone had to wait or by asking the work crew to operate on a "drop-everything-and-fix-this-one" schedule. The supervisor might quietly have done things to screw up the drivers' work in a form of silent revenge. All of these things produce a sense of satisfaction for the concealer, but they hurt the company.

Suppose the small motor supervisor were an avoider. If he decided that there was no solution to the problem, and if he decided to avoid any kind of problem with the drivers, the whole small motor shop might have suffered, especially if the problem was just transferred to the lower level workers. There might have been times when it was necessary for the supervisor to tell the drivers, "Enough is enough. We are too busy right now, so don't promise anything tomorrow, because it won't be finished." If the supervisor couldn't talk to the drivers in such a way, life would have been made miserable for the supervisor and for the crew. If the supervisor were a "quitter," the shop would have suffered by losing his services. So whatever type the supervisor was, the organization would have suffered.

Thus, there is no "right way to be," or right type of person to hire to avoid conflict. In a world in which people respond to situations in different ways, we must keep in mind that all the ways of responding can produce difficult side effects for an organization. It might seem that the best situation would be a group of addressers, but this is an illusion. There is no reason to believe that addressers would hit on a solution. It is too easy to spend your time talking about everyone's hurt feelings and not getting anywhere near a real solution.

The point of this chapter has been to introduce the cast of characters in conflict situations and some of the strategies that people use to protect themselves when faced with conflicts. A few hard truths about conflict situations should be remembered. One is that the ways in which people respond to conflict situations tend to obscure the conflicts. The fact that some people are up front about their feelings or have "constructive" attitudes doesn't necessarily mean that the conflicts are on the way to resolution. The people who are blamed often just end up doing their jobs less well or creating problems for themselves.

Another hard truth about conflict situations is that our ordinary vocabulary of "blame" frequently misleads us. Tactics for obscuring responsibility and avoiding blame are common, and they are common because they work. They are accepted, and when they are accepted, they take the heat off of someone. When they are used, they often mislead everyone, including the people they protect, who think that the ambiguities and blocks are real facts of life in the organization.

The chapter can be summed up in one rule. In a conflict situation, don't ask "who?"; ask "what?" and "why?" Asking "who?" may get you a convenient answer, namely, that so-and-so is to blame, but the answer is almost always an illusion. The idea that if the "troublemakers" can be eliminated the trouble will be eliminated is almost always wrong, because the trouble is usually a matter of the blocking and covering tactics used by people whose response style is such that they are incapable of making visible "trouble" that catches the eye in a conflict situation. The "underground" tactics almost always hurt the organization more than the public trouble, and should be the manager's primary concern.

2

THE MYTH OF THE GROUCHY BOSS

Trouble in organizations is contagious: A single unhappy boss can spread conflict through an organization like an epidemic disease, so poisoning the atmosphere with tension that experienced and cooperative workers—especially the nonconfronters and avoiders we discussed in the last chapter—may reach a point where they feel their jobs have become intolerable. These workers may suddenly quit.

The most serious difficulties for the organization occur when a conflict involves a person's blocking the actions of other people. Blocking can take the form of overt hostility or of a quiet passive resistance. Conflict can result when a person is grouchy and irritable all the time, blocking the work of other people who avoid dealing with him or her for fear of provoking hostility, or it can be caused by the kind of passive resistance in which the person never seems to cooperate or get anything done, thereby impeding the smooth running of the organization. In either case, conflicts block actions, increase tensions, and cut productivity.

HOW WE TALK ABOUT PROBLEM PEOPLE

"Personality Clashes"

For the employees of an organization, the grouchy and irritable boss or fellow worker is no myth. Those individuals who are hostile or troublesome to deal with are real enough to the people who have to work with them. Yet often our ways of talking about the behavior of these people obscures the reasons for their behavior. If you ask, "Why don't people cooperate more around here?" the tendency is to point out certain individuals who cause hostility and tension and excuse their behavior by saying there is simply a personality clash between this boss and the workers or between two workers. The idea of a personality clash may be based on our perception that these individuals want an independent say in how they will do their work, or that they are simply aggressive and competitive people. In short, the explanation for why individuals cause conflict and tension often focuses on personality traits.

The idea that organizational conflict is caused by personality traits of a few people in an organization is a convenient way for people to describe the conflict they experience, but it does not tell us much about the ways in which we might *change* the situation for the better. In this sense, the idea that conflict is caused by a personality clash represents a set of ideas or a myth that often hides the aspects of the situation that *can* be changed to eliminate the conflict.

A good place to begin in correcting our thinking about these people is to ask some questions about the "problem people." We may notice that supervisors and workers who are difficult to get along with and who cause conflict on the job are likeable and easygoing away from the job. One might ask the logical question, *If the cause of the conflict is the individuals' personalities, then why are they not difficult to get along with all the time?* Other useful questions to ask concern a problem person's beliefs: Does the person think that the way he or she is doing the job is the way it has to be done or should be done? Are there some understandable reasons for his or her beliefs? Is the person frustrated? These questions suggest that there must be something in the work situation that causes the problem.

In this chapter we will consider some examples of cases that can be described in personality terms but that can be *better* described in situational, nonpersonality, terms.

Varieties of Conflict Behavior

One extreme type of conflict behavior is the expression of hostility. At the opposite extreme is quiet passive resistance. Between these extremes are a number of kinds of conflict behavior, all of which are commonly found in organizations:

1. irritability
2. flashes of anger
3. demandingness and uncooperativeness
4. self-centeredness and lack of concern for others
5. hiding behind operating rules, doing everything "by-the-book," which is related to
6. the "I won't do it because I'll get blamed for it" syndrome.

All of these represent a blockage in the process of cooperation among workers.

The most hostile of these kinds of behavior, in which a person shows a general irritability toward everyone, serves as a way of keeping other people from making demands on the person. A person who does this can reduce problems of conflicting demands by making it difficult for anyone to ask him to do anything. Flashes of anger, or "blow-ups," from the supervisor with intermittent periods in which he seems to be friendly to everyone, frequently occurs in organizations in which the work flow is erratic or unpredictable but in which the supervisor has deadlines to meet. This kind of situation causes workers to believe that the boss has a terrible temper—as a personality trait, even though during periods of stress people ordinarily react with flashes of anger. The pressure of the work demands in such a situation may be so great that almost anyone would find it difficult to keep a cool head.

When a supervisor suddenly becomes uncompromising and demanding, such behavior may be caused by his or her tremendous responsibility for getting a job done but little control over all the factors that are needed to get it done. Consider, for example, the problem of a caterer putting on a dinner for a large group of people. Timing is crucial—if something is late, the pace of the meal is disturbed; other dishes must be delayed and may lose quality by drying out, warming, or cooling. Yet many things may happen that produce small delays, and once one thing gets out of synchronization the whole process begins to become chaotic. Waiters end up waiting for dishes and not serving them. People who aren't served, or who are served cold food and warm drinks, become angry and demanding. So the caterer is pushed into being demanding and uncompromising in supervising the work of other people because this is the only place where he or she has any real control.

Passive resistance behavior may appear to us as extreme self-centeredness and a lack of concern for the feelings of others. This sort of response can occur in competitive situations in which workers must compete for bonuses or good evaluations. Competition tends to make people self-centered and uncooperative. Unnecessary competition often builds up in a work situation in which individual productivity is rewarded more than is group productivity. In many cases productivity would be increased if people were free to cooperate with one another.

Finally, workers or supervisors may hide behind the rules. They will want everything done "by the book," even if it means that the work is not done effectively. The underlying reason may be that these workers or supervisors are afraid to assume responsibility, thereby eliciting the "I'll get blamed for it" syndrome. In either the by-the-book or "I'll get blamed for it" situation, these forms of passive resistance tend to create hostility in other workers when they are blocked from doing their jobs effectively. Sometimes the "hiding behind the rules" or the "I'll get blamed for it" syndrome occurs because people feel that they are being passed by or are not being consulted about matters that are their responsibility. One way they avoid being passed over is by insisting that all the operating rules be followed and that everything go through channels so that they feel they are a necessary part of the organization. If such people felt more secure in their jobs, they would no doubt act more cooperatively and effectively.

If we look beyond individual personality clashes or troublesome personality traits and focus our attention on the *situations* that leave people without a sense of confidence and well-being, we begin to talk about organizational conflicts in ways that enable us to solve them. Yet it is difficult for most people to look beyond the troublesome individual and focus on the troublesome situation.

The fact that a wide range of individual differences can be seen in people's responses and expressions of their feelings and frustrations in situations that can cause organizational conflict is one source of the difficulty. Because different people behave differently in the same troublesome situation, it appears that the conflict behavior is entirely a matter of the individual's personality and not of the work situation. Because the same situation does not *always* produce the same individual response, we tend to discount the significance of the situation. For one person, a troublesome situation may produce storms of anger followed by periods of relative calm during which the pressures of the situation cause storm clouds to build again. For another person, the identical situation may cause him or her to act in a self-centered way by belittling others and avoiding responsibility. Organizational situations bring out different reactions from different people because they have learned different ways of coping with their frustrations.

Once we have trained ourselves to look for the troublesome situation, it is possible to eliminate the organizational conflict regardless of how the individuals express their frustration. Situations that produce conflict are quite varied, but they are often easy to spot once we begin to look for them. The following sections show some important types of situations.

Work Overload

In some work situations, a person has too much to do in too short a period of time. Work overload can occur when work is not well coordinated or when clear priorities about what needs to be finished first have not been made. Supervisors often respond at such times with hostility, which is caused by the tension created in the work situation. Work overload almost always produces several different kinds of conflict behavior among individual workers and supervisors, ranging from blow-ups or flashes of anger to a slowing down of the work process by the insistence that everything be done "by the book." Resentment on the part of some members of the organization against other members inevitably results. People accuse others of working too slowly or being ineffective in their jobs, and a thick atmosphere of tension clouds the work setting.

One of the best examples of a place where work overload becomes a problem is in a restaurant, where the rush of customers at mealtimes can create a demanding and frustrating work situation. Various studies have shown that when the work flow and layout of a restaurant are carefully structured, these overload situations are handled without undue frustration, but when the work flow is not structured and cooks and waitresses are required to do too many varied tasks, conflict erupts.

Work Underload

It seems improbable that a situation in which people have too little to do can cause much organizational conflict; however, when people have too little to do they tend to feel unimportant. Boredom, inactivity, and a sense of unimportance can produce conflict behaviors as readily as can work overload. There is some truth in the old saying, "If you keep people busy they will stay out of trouble."

People without enough work to do can cause trouble by looking for work in other people's work areas. A dispute may erupt as to whose responsibility it is for getting particular tasks done. Workers may, in an effort to establish self-importance, try to take over other people's jobs, which can lead to jealousies and produce conflict.

In some work underload situations, conflict occurs when workers perceive other workers as sitting around and doing nothing. If two groups of workers are paid the same amount of money and are supposed to share the same amount of responsibility, then the workers who have the most work to do will be upset by the inactivity of the other workers. Serious morale problems can develop; the fact that the group that suffers work underload has not been asked to do more work is generally overlooked. The group with the lighter workload will simply be seen as lazy and irresponsible and will have to suffer the contempt of fellow workers.

Conflicting Demands

Demands "conflict" when two different jobs must be done at the same time and yet the doing of the one job automatically prevents the doing of the other job. As an example, a manufacturing situation may have pressure for high production and at the same time the need for machine maintenance. If machine maintenance requires that the machines be shut down for a long period of time, this will reduce production. At the same time, if the machines are not maintained they will break down, preventing a high production rate. A department supervisor who feels pressure to keep high production levels may create a situation of conflicting demands between the need for machine maintenance and the need for high production. These conflicting demands can cause flashes of hostility among the workers and scapegoating when the production rates begin to fall. To the people in the situation, it will look like *someone* is to blame, when the situation itself is to blame.

Responsibility Without Control

A supervisor may, according to his or her evaluations and job description, be responsible for seeing that a job is done quickly, efficiently, and inexpensively; however, the supervisor's success may totally depend on the job performance of people who are not accountable to the supervisor for their work. In a situation in which the supervisor is given the burden of responsibility without being given the power to control the work for which he or she is responsible, that supervisor may become the stereotypical "grouchy boss," making demands on the people he or she has control over, displaying impatience at delays, becoming difficult to get along with, and complaining bitterly about the work of the people over which he or she has no control. The complaints and criticisms themselves are frequently the cause of more trouble. The situation is often relatively easy to fix: Reduce the supervisor's responsibility and give some of it back to those people who control the actual work, thereby making the supervisor feel more in control of the job for which he or she is responsible. Unfortunately, the situational problem is often misdescribed and misunderstood as a personnel problem. The supervisor is evaluated as being unable to get along with people and as having a nervous and irritable personality that causes people to avoid contact with him or her, which thereby reduces the cooperation and effectiveness required to do the job.

Win-lose Situations

By setting up a competitive system of rewards in the form of win-lose situations, organizations create a work atmosphere that fosters personal conflicts. The win-lose situation begins with the identification of certain people as being the best at their job. The best workers may be identified by their rate of sales, as making the fewest mistakes, or as having the highest productivity, or by some other method of rank ordering people's performance. When these people are then given rewards for their work, such as favorable personnel ratings, bonuses, merit raises, and promotions, then very often workers begin to compete with one another and to regard their jobs not so much as tasks to be accomplished well but as a competition to be won. What is often lost sight of in this competition is that workers who perform their job adequately and could not easily be replaced may still be seen as the worst workers in the group, because in a win-lose situation somebody is always a loser. A salesperson who sells a million dollars' worth of merchandise a year and who may in ordinary terms be considered as a very good salesperson may still be seen as the poorest salesperson in the group because his colleagues have sold *more* than a million dollars' worth of merchandise in a year.

The win-lose situation becomes even more desperate when the success of one person has to be based on the failure of another person. For example, imagine a situation where a group of workers must assemble products (say radios) each day from the available supply of parts, and when all the parts are used up they are sent home. In this situation, competition will be created by paying the workers on the basis of the number of finished products they produce in a day. In such a situation the faster workers, in an effort to make more money, are using up the parts that could be available to the slower workers, thereby decreasing the possible daily income of slower workers. This is a situation where the faster workers are directly penalizing the slower workers. In this kind of a win-lose situation, slower workers might become hostile to the faster workers, and they might engage in various troublesome behaviors to try to slow them down. In addition, the slower workers might try to stockpile parts in their work areas in order to prevent the faster workers from using up these parts. At the same time, the faster workers might feel that the parts belong to everyone and that therefore they should have a right to them. In any event, this kind of win-lose situation creates enormous interpersonal tension and hostility. The tendency is for people to interpret this win-lose situation as a series of personality clashes. The slower workers view the faster workers as very competitive, self-centered, and uncooperative. The faster workers, on the other hand, view the slower workers as troublemakers or chronic complainers.

Many of these problems could be easily solved by changing the system of rewards in the situation from individual bonus payments to a system of group bonus payments. Win-lose situations almost always produce troublesome side effects. Because we commonly use competition to motivate people in organizations, it is important to be aware of and to avoid or prevent some of the destructive conflict that competitive situations create. Where win-lose competition is not necessary, it should be eliminated, and where competition can't be eliminated, it should be transformed from individual competition to group competition.

Line and Staff Conflict

The terms "line" and "staff" have been used to describe two different groups of employees in a business organization. Line employees are members of the organization who have authority and responsibility that is concerned with the main production operation of the company. They hold such titles as general manager, division chief, department chief, superintendent, and supervisor, and they are primarily concerned with the control and coordination of the basic operations of the company. The staff consists of individuals who perform specialized functions and are considered to be experts in one particular area, such as engineers, accountants, or members of the research and development department. These two different administrative groups should complement each other in the operation of the firm, with line officials drawing on the expert knowledge of the staff employees. Yet the workings of these two groups often produce difficult problems of conflict between the different employees.

First, we should note that line employees have more authority and prestige and tend to make more money in salary than staff employees. Staff employees, on the other hand, as experts in a particular area, tend to believe that their views as to how the company should be run should prevail. Yet staff employees often feel they must prove themselves in order to gain acceptance. These differences form the basis for ongoing conflicts between line and staff employees. Because there is no agreement as to the best way to integrate the staff and line functions of an organization, many different forms of conflict tend to arise. These conflicts are sometimes heightened because staff people not only consider themselves part of the management but also feel that their technical knowledge makes them superior to the line officials.

The actual conflict between the two groups usually focuses on superficial differences between them and draws attention away from the more fundamental problem. For example, staff employees are often younger than line employees, so that conflict focuses on age differences. For instance, when line officials fail to act on their suggestions, staff employees may react with angry remarks about how the line officials are "a bunch of ignorant old goats" or "bull-headed geezers." At the same time the line officials may feel that the staff people are a bunch of "impractical whiz-kids" who don't really understand how the company works.

The conflict between line and staff can also focus on the difference between knowledge based on experience and knowledge based on technical education, such that staff people do not respect the line officers' experience and the line people do not respect the staff's formal education in terms of their ability to solve practical problems.

When staff employees feel frustrated because they cannot get their suggestions implemented by the line officials, they might try a different approach. For instance, they might search out a sympathetic line official and take their ideas there for a favorable hearing. In doing so, however, the staff employees would earn the reputation of being sneaky and of short-circuiting the channels of communication. This would only serve to heighten the distrust of their immediate line supervisor who might react by starting a crackdown that would tighten control and create even more friction.

Some of this inherent conflict between line and staff employees in an organization can be reduced by clearly specifying when the staff may have some authority over the operations of the company and by assigning to line officials staff assistants who are charged with working closely with the line officer. Unfortunately, line and staff conflicts are not easily controlled by simply changing work assignments, although some arrangements might be easier to live with than others.

Dead-end Jobs

How many companies create, at all levels, dead-end jobs? The number must be astronomical. Dead-end jobs are jobs that have a flat career line. That is, 1) there are no promotions, 2) there is no guarantee of a regular raise in pay, and 3) there is no real change in the routine of the job. The only thing a worker in a dead-end job has to look forward to is not working: the worker looks forward to the weekend, holidays, and ultimately retirement. In a dead-end job the employee works just enough to avoid being fired. The job demands very little of an employee, and usually that person feels no obligation or encouragement to give anything more than this bare minimum to the job. Nevertheless, the company expects people in such jobs to work faithfully, without any problems, day-in, day-out, and year-in, year-out.

Dead-end jobs create some conflict problems, brought about by the workers' feelings of unimportance, frustration, and boredom. The most characteristic effects of a dead-end job are low work satisfaction and poor motivation. Workers in this situation do their work grudgingly and also tend to "put their job on hold," doing as little as possible to get by. They do this not because they are lazy, but because they have come to share the contempt for the job that others in the organization feel. Another reaction that some workers in dead-end jobs manifest is chronic forgetfulness and seemingly endless foul-ups. This makes workers in dead-end jobs unreliable, which causes difficulties for everyone around them. Perhaps they don't keep their minds on their work because their jobs are really not worth thinking about.

Other employee reactions to dead-end jobs can be categorized under the heading "seeking self-importance." For example, employees in dead-end jobs may become people who don't seem to do any work without other people giving them a lot of personal attention. These are the kind of people to whom you cannot just send a memorandum, but you must hand-carry it to their office, explain the memorandum, and then spend time listening to all the details of their children's sports, music, and school events. This need for personal attention becomes the prime element in the employees' job satisfaction, so that they cannot do the job without the attention. Another way that employees in dead-end jobs may seek self-importance is to block the work of other people by requiring that they follow all the rules without exception. This rule-following ritualism makes those employees feel important, but at the same time it may slow up company output by days or even weeks. Finally, people in dead-end jobs may be angry and resentful about the position that they are in, and therefore they may enhance their sense of self-importance by fault finding and belittling others.

How are dead-end jobs created? Often they are created unintentionally, through decisions whose side-effects are not realized at the time. Consider what can happen if a particular kind of work experience becomes a requirement for promotion. Something like this happened in the Air Force in its early days, when combat flying experience was necessary for promotion. Once a job is deemed unimportant experience for a future top manager, then it may come to be regarded by other employees in the company as a dead-end job. Some of the problems of dead-end jobs can be solved by a job rotation scheme linked to regular pay raises or bonuses over a period of time. In this way, employees can develop some sense of career, and the company does not have to promote everyone to be vice-president.

These organizational situations are fairly commonplace ones, and social scientists have spent a considerable amount of time researching the situational conditions that are related to people's individual reactions to work situations. There are, of course, other work situations with potential to cause conflict of which you should be aware. To discover the situational problems of the work setting, start with looking beyond the troublesome person or persons, and focus your attention on the total situation. Then ask, "What are people in this situation being asked to do?" and, "What satisfaction can they be getting from doing what they are doing?" Your answers to these questions may seem paradoxical at first. For example, you might decide that "He is making everyone's life miserable so he can feel like he is liked and included in things." Don't let the paradoxical situation throw you off. You may be right, and there are things that can be tried in an effort to find a solution to this and many other kinds of problems.

This chapter has shown some of the ways in which conflict results from the organizational setting and not from the personality traits of supervisors and workers. People in organizations create an explanation of conflict that centers the problem on the "troublesome individual." This is what we have called the myth of the grouchy boss. Any worker may be grouchy, uncooperative, and temperamental, but the causes of this conflict behavior often lie in the work situation and not in the personality of the individual. We do not mean to say that there is no such thing as a personality problem, and we certainly do not mean to say that grouchiness is not a real experience for the person who is reprimanded by a hostile boss. We do mean to say that describing a problem as a "personality problem" or a "personnel problem" can be a misleading way of describing it. The situation the person is in often tells part or all of the story of why he or she is grouchy or unpleasant. Learning to read *situations* as well as *people* is a basic competency for anyone who wants to understand how organizations work. In the next chapter we will be discussing the development of these skills.

3

HIDDEN CONSEQUENCES OF CONFLICT

In Chapter 1 we looked at the way people feel in conflict situations, and we gave a few hints about the ways that these feelings come to be misdirected, as in the case of the small motor supervisor's open hostility toward the truck drivers. In Chapter 2 we looked at some typical situations that make for conflict in organizations, and we established that troublesome situations tend to create troublesome individuals and that it is the situation, not the individual, that needs to be dealt with. In Chapter 4 we will talk systematically about the diagnosis of conflict-prone structures; in the next chapter we will talk about changing them. Before doing these things we need to put the lessons of Chapter 1 and Chapter 2 together.

An important lesson of Chapter 1 was that feelings and public, overt responses aren't a very good guide to what conflicts are about, because people respond to problem situations in a variety of ways which conceal the conflicts or blame the most convenient person. Chapter 2 taught us that situations produce conflict. The problem with talking about "situations" is that, in practice, spotting the conflict situation requires more than simply looking at job descriptions or job assignments. It involves seeing how people are actually responding to their job assignments. When we use a term such as work overload, for example, we are making a practical judgment about what is or isn't "too much." Or when we talk about conflicting demands, we need to recognize that this does not merely mean that a variety of different demands have been placed on a worker at any given time; almost all jobs involve this. We need to judge whether these demands conflict as well. Just asking the employees whether the demands on them conflict or whether they have too much work won't settle the questions either. Imagine your response if your boss dropped by and asked what the problem was about some task, or asked something that sounds like, "Is this job too much for you?" You would just point the finger, or take the blame yourself and try harder, or deny that there was a problem, according to your style of responding to that kind of situation. In later chapters we will discuss the problem of fear and trust when questions like these are asked. For now, all we need to do is notice that the usual responses to questions aren't enough to give us the total picture.

The relationship between situations and people's emotions is a complex one. It can be illustrated by spending a minute to analyze the intent of a practical joke. To play a practical joke, we set up a situation for someone and then stand back and watch the emotional reaction of embarrassment, frustration, anger, and so on. To create a good practical joke, you must change a situation in such a way that the victims will not recognize that the situation is in fact different from the way they perceive it. Some of us will admit to having played, in our extreme youth, the old practical joke of putting salt in the sugar bowl. All we had to do was sit back and watch our victims, our parents, act in their normal way, which in this situation was by putting sugar in their coffee. The joke comes about when the victims discover the incongruity between what they thought they had done and the outcome—what they taste when they drink their coffee. The fact that practical jokes are one of the most risky forms of humor shows that individuals do not like to deal with incongruities between what they want and expect in a situation and what the situation actually delivers. Our jobs can be one prolonged "practical joke," in which we must work out different ways of coping with the situation.

How do you recognize situations in which the degree of stress and pressure has become a problem? The best place to start in recognizing problem situations is to notice the coping behavior. A simple example is complaining. When employees air their complaints about someone—stand around the water cooler and gripe about the boss, or the salespeople, or the dietician, or whomever—they are coping. Ignore for a moment the contents of the complaints. Who or what they blame for their troubles may well be irrelevant to the solution of the problem. The way they cope does not necessarily have anything directly to do with the source of their troubles; think of coping as a symptom, just as coughing and sneezing are symptoms of a cold. Remember, symptoms often are the things of a disease that kill you. In organizations, the coping behavior may be extremely damaging, especially when it involves blocking the work of others in the organization. Sometimes the coping is not obstructive in itself, but is obstructive in its effects. When a person with many responsibilities copes with some of them by giving them a low priority or by studiously ignoring problems that come up in the hope that they will go away, the consequences may also be serious.

Just looking around the organization won't necessarily tell you who is coping, because some people may exhibit their coping behavior during their off hours at home. They may go home and kick their dog, or fight with their spouse, or chain smoke; all of these can be coping behavior. But by recognizing coping behavior where it is visible, and by using the clues properly, you can usually identify trouble spots. In this chapter we will be concerned with how to recognize trouble spots by noticing coping behavior. There can be no neat rules for identifying coping, so the best way to learn is by considering examples.

CASE A: THE WORD PROCESSING UNIT

The Situation

In a junior college it was decided that it would be practical and efficient to develop separate word processing units in each building. Most but not all of the buildings had offices and classrooms, and this arrangement made it easier for the teachers. This situation worked nicely enough. Productivity criteria and expected workload were developed, and each unit was allocated personnel and overtime on the basis of need. It also seemed like a good idea for the audiovisual people to store movie projectors and other equipment in each building and the word processing employees to be responsible for carting projectors to the classrooms as needed. Because the only unit that was represented in each building was the word processing center, it seemed like a good idea to make the word processing center the clearinghouse for requests for audiovisual equipment and give the word processing employees the responsibility for making sure that the right equipment was in the right classroom. This task had to be performed only a few times a day, at the beginning of a class period. There was not enough work spread out over the day to justify hiring one person to do the job in each of the buildings, and the word processing center could adjust its work schedule to meet the needs of the added task.

This simple solution was a recipe for trouble. No sooner did the system start than the workers in the word processing center and the supervisors of each unit became upset. But they coped. They blamed the people who complained when there wasn't enough audiovisual equipment to go around, and they envied the lucky people in buildings where there was no audiovisual equipment to interfere with their normal work. Some of the workers tried to get transferred to one of those buildings.

No one complained to the higher level supervisor of the word processing units because the problem was not a word processing problem but an audiovisual problem, something over which the supervisor of the word processing units had no real authority. When the workers complained to the supervisor of the audiovisual section of the college, they were told that the college could not afford to hire special personnel to work the hour a day that it takes to get equipment to the right place in each of their buildings.

The Feelings

The employees in the word processing units were miserable. Some of them quit as soon as they were trained and could find another job, and others transferred to units that didn't have audiovisual equipment. Most of the workers in the word processing units with audiovisual equipment ended up to be new trainees, then, and of course efficiency went down. The word processing supervisors of the buildings with audiovisual equipment complained about the audiovisual unit supervisor. They had no control over that person, so they coped until there wasn't room to cope any more. Yet no one knew exactly what was wrong. Everything seemed "necessary" and "rational" and therefore had to be coped with.

The expectations that everyone had at every point in the process were "reasonable." The teachers needed their projectors, and the higher level word processing supervisor expected the unit supervisors in each building to have their units produce all the necessary paperwork in quantities that corresponded to the number of employees and the number of hours a day that the employees worked. The audiovisual equipment wasn't the higher level word processing supervisor's responsibility, and there was nothing she could do about it. The building unit supervisors, or at least those with audiovisual responsibilities, felt tremendous stress. Where they felt it was in their daily relations with teachers; that is what they wanted to fix. The teacher-unit supervisor contact was what we can call a *pressure point*, a term we will discuss in the next chapter. The teacher-unit supervisor relationship was the relationship of conflict irritation and the problem for daily coping. The more coping everyone on each side had to do, the more difficult the situation became. Sooner or later this irritant began to interfere with the word processing work that was done for the teachers, because the resentment became associated with the people the word processing employees had to deal with.

Having someone higher up in authority adjudicate problems one by one in such a case would have been hopeless. In the word processing example, if anyone wanted to take their complaints to a higher-up they would have had to go to the vice-president! The vice-president was the first person one would reach who was the supervising officer of *both* the word processing and the audiovisual supervisors. This illustrates a particularly common and bad organizational strategy. If a problem can only be settled by someone as far up the ladder past the problem as the vice-president is, it will never be solved. Assigning a problem to a vice-president, as is often done, is largely useful as a way of stifling problems without solving them. In general, when responsibility for a problem is shifted to higher-ups, this is like saying "shut up" to the people involved. No one in their right mind would bring a problem as specific as the problem over scheduling a piece of audiovisual equipment to a vice-president. Going to a higher-up on matters like this is almost admitting incompetence. Regardless of how just your case is, bringing up the problem is going to make you look like a complainer, troublemaker, or shirker. Coping is easier, even if coping means quitting.

The Organizational Problem

There is a lesson to be discovered from the fact that organizations use the tactic of assigning responsibility to people in ways that assure that the responsibilities aren't carried out. The goals of the higher-ups don't include such trivial matters as getting the audiovisual equipment handled properly. They regard such matters as significant only if these matters become problems and get in the way of the goals that *they* are held accountable for, namely, things that involve numbers and budgets. These are the things that they can understand, because these are what they are paid to understand by their superiors. For them, as for their subordinates, the world is divided up between things that help and things that hinder. The people who dump their problems on the vice-president's desk are hindrances. Employees at every level, including the top, know this and accordingly hide their problems from those above them. If you want a model of this, think about how honest, forthright, and candid the president and board of a corporation are at a shareholders meeting. They act just about like any other subordinate: everything's under control, there are no real problems, at least that can't be handled, and so forth.

If the people with the problem do complain to the people above them, they often do so in self-defeating ways. They apologize too much, they get too angry, they appear selfish or lazy, or discredit themselves in any of a dozen other ways. If, as more often happens, they don't complain, they go on resenting the people with whom they have the problem, in this case the teachers who want the audiovisual equipment. Because this isn't noticeable to anyone outside or above the people involved, it isn't considered to be a problem until something happens that is obviously and clearly contrary to the goals of the top administrative officers.

So the lesson is this: Organizations have many ways of getting people to swallow their complaints. What usually happens in conflict situations is that the standard means of getting people to shut up don't seem to work, and the stresses that were always there become a "problem," that is, the conflict becomes visible and makes the relationships with other people difficult. Of course, organizations and the people in them can suffer considerably long before that point is reached, so in order to deal effectively with conflict, a manager has to be able to deal with conflicts that haven't surfaced as well as deal with those conflicts that have become a visible problem. In this situation, a good way to spot the problem would be to notice which people have quit or changed jobs within the organization and where they have transferred from. There is a term for this. The proportion of people quitting a job over a given period of time is called the "quit rate." Stressful jobs tend to have the highest quit rates. Another similar sign of a stressful job is the number of sick days or unaccounted absences that are recorded within a work unit.

The difficulty with all these symptoms and signs is that every one can be the result of something besides stress caused by the structure of the situation. People may quit because the pay is too low or because the only opportunity for advancement comes by taking another job. Some jobs tend to be filled by people who have other conflicts: Parents with primary nurturing responsibility of school-age children usually must spend a lot of time off work taking them to doctors or caring for them at home; people with young families are often under such financial pressure that salary increases, however minor, loom very large, so they are more likely to quit a job if they think they can get slightly higher wages in another job. Because the behavior that is associated with stressful jobs can also be caused by situations outside of the job, the symptoms we have talked about here are never fool-proof signs of stressful jobs.

When we say "often this" and "frequently that," it reflects the fact that any given symptom is subject to various interpretations. More than one of the interpretations may be true and none of the symptoms always means the work situation is at fault. Moreover, just as there is more than one way to skin a cat, there is more than one way for people in a bad situation to cope with it. A person's way of coping may also serve purposes other than those it appears to serve. By fighting over the audiovisual equipment, people may be coping with their home life conflicts, just as they might be coping with their office conflicts by arguing with their spouses. Stated differently, situations are like balloons: When you press them in, they must push out someplace else. With people, you can see where the "pushing out" occurs, but you can't tell what is the source of the "pressing in." It takes a little careful detective work to discover where the problem begins.

CASE B: THE COCOA DISTRIBUTOR

The Situation

A small firm produces and distributes cocoa for institutions. The largest contracts are primarily with restaurant chains. There are two sides to the business: production and sales. The general manager with experience in both sides of the business is the boss, and the two sales managers and the director of operations report to him. He reports to the owners—operators who have many holdings yet spend time at the company and generally try to keep an eye on the business first-hand. They hired the general manager because he had experience in the business, and they transferred the director of operations from the home office, where he had gotten a lot of financial experience.

One day one of the sales managers came in to the general manager's office to complain about a problem. Packages were being filled with the wrong weight of cocoa so that when they were dumped into the automatic cocoa machine the mix was either too strong or too weak. Customers were complaining to the company about the cocoa and the salespeople were getting complaints and threats. The general manager went down to the loading dock to ask about the situation and was told by one employee, on the side, that a whole batch of cocoa had been mispackaged, but that the director of operations knew it and ordered them to send it out anyway. The general manager then marched up to the director of operations and told him what had been discovered and asked that it never be done again. Amazingly, the director of operations denied that any cocoa had been mispackaged.

The general manager investigated as far as possible during the next week. As far as he could determine, the director of operations had lied. Another talk with the director of operations, stressing the importance of quality control, proved to be no more successful. The director of operations simply said, in effect, "There is no problem. There never has been a problem; you just have bad information."

The Feelings

A war of nerves between the general manager and the director of operations began. The lie, if it was a lie, made the general manager suspicious of everything the director of operations said. The director of operations became more touchy about questions. Every question seemed a personal attack on his competence. When the owners showed up, the general manager wasn't sure what to do. The owners had a longstanding relationship with the director of operations, and the director of operations was in fact there as the financial eyes and ears of the owners. Whenever the owners came to visit, they spent hours together huddled over the books. The owners wouldn't fire the director of operations on just the general manager's say-so.

The effects of the problem didn't show up in the director of operations's side of the business. The books showed that operations were running as cheaply and as productively as ever. Sales, on the other hand, were off a bit because a few big contracts were lost, but whose fault was that? As far as the owners could see, it was probably the sales managers' fault.

The problem here sounds simple because a lie seems like such an unambiguous thing, something that's just plain wrong. Our sympathies are all with the general manager. But this shouldn't distract us from the realization that the director of operations, though he seems to be in an enviable position, is really in a very unpleasant one. He can't admit making the mistake, especially with the owners around all the time, because it is his relationship with the owners that landed him the job in the first place, not his relationship with the general manager. Admitting the mistake would give the general manager power to discredit him in the eyes of the owners. He knows that the general manager may decide to use it that way, because it would get the general manager off the hook for the fall in sales, which is ordinarily the responsibility of that officer. The general manager may also be jealous and suspicious of the director of operations's relationship with the owners. So lying about what happened, as bewildering as it seems, has a kind of logic to it.

The Organizational Consequences

A lie shifts the burden of doing something onto another person and in conflict situations, as we saw in the last case, the one who complains first always raises the question, *Who is the real problem here, anyway?* In this particular case, the risk for the general manager of complaining, of being the first to bring the issue into the open, is pretty serious. What if the owners believe the director of operations and not the general manager?

The relationship between the general manager and the director of operations is at a stalemate. The problem will probably never reach the owners simply because the risks on each side are too high. It has consequences nevertheless. The day-to-day relationship won't involve much trust, so it will take a lot of additional effort on both sides to check out the other's activities and intentions, because each has reason to fear that the owners will side with the other. Also, the degree of honesty with the owners is bound to decrease.

The same lesson applies to almost any conflict that hasn't surfaced. The protective mechanisms that people have available to them almost always hurt the organization—bad information, time spent on keeping up a good front instead of on work, time spent on the rumor mill, and decisions made out of vulnerability and fear. In this case, the general manager would be very hesitant to make a proposal that the director of operations could sabotage and then use for discrediting purposes. The director of operations would make decisions that would hurt the general manager most. The decision to send out the mispackaged cocoa was exactly this sort of decision, and it did hurt the company (but of course not in a way that could be traced to the director of operations).

So communication between the general manager and the director of operations has been filled with suspicion. Innocent behavior that is just part of doing the job in the company is now viewed as sinister or malicious. The problem is now hidden and can only be detected by observing the cool avoidance practices of the general manager and the director of operations. Avoidance is not easy to detect, because it can be disguised as being "too busy to get together." Nevertheless the problem may manifest itself in little ways that further depress sales so that the general manager's competence will be called into question by the owners of the company.

CASE C: THE WAREHOUSE WORKERS

The Situation

A large retail company has a central warehousing operation. The firm is an older, well-managed firm that boasts of its track record of good labor-management relations. The top managers of the company discovered that some of its employees had stolen a large amount of merchandise while their supervisors had stood by unperturbed. The theft had been detected by the accounting department in a routine audit, and with some investigation by the top managers, it was revealed that the supervisor in the warehousing branch must have known that the thefts had occurred because of the amount and kind of merchandise stolen. The executives were astonished. They had thought that their supervisors were loyal company men and that they had been treated fairly. They didn't understand how such thievery could take place in their company.

The Organizational Problem

We don't usually think of stealing as an organizational problem, but when the first-line supervisors look the other way so that stealing can go on, it then becomes more than an individual problem; it becomes an organizational problem. Understanding theft as an organizational problem requires us to focus on the problem of why people don't feel responsible. It's apparent that the warehouse supervisors should be the ones responsible for preventing theft where possible, or at least they should be responsible for reporting thefts and trying to solve the crimes so that the thieves can be fired. If this is so, then why didn't the supervisors feel responsible? After all, it is part of their job to maintain some minimum standards of discipline in the work situation. To understand this problem we must first understand how the erosion of control in the work situation affected what actions the supervisors could take and how they felt about their position in the organization. When you erode away control of the work situation from individuals, you also indirectly erode away the individuals' feelings of responsibility for what goes on in the work situation. In this situation we need to notice a few other things.

The company had renegotiated its union contract every two years. Obviously the appropriate person to handle the negotiations was the vice-president in charge of personnel and labor relations. After all, top union officials prefer to negotiate with top management officials. However, the supervisors of the various sections of the company, who were responsible for carrying out a new union contract, were never asked how they felt about the contract or what problems they had in implementing a contract. So, although the workers were represented by their union, the supervisors were not represented by management. Furthermore, by its action, management effectively communicated to the supervisors that they didn't matter much to the operations of the company. An additional sore point was created by the fact that the union let grievances pile up, knowing full well that management would settle them all in the union's favor just to get a contract as quickly as possible. Many of these grievances arose when supervisors tried to carry out the terms of the previous contract, so when management gave in easily, the supervisors felt that they had been double-crossed. In effect, the supervisors were being told that they didn't have anything useful to contribute to company policy, that their job was to do as they were told, and that they were expendable whenever necessary. The vice-president in charge of labor relations did not intend to create hard feelings, but by leaving their problems and concerns out of the contract negotiations with the union, she effectively undercut the status and authority of the supervisors.

The Organizational Consequences

By turning the other way when employees stole merchandise, the lower level management—the supervisors—made the workers feel obliged to them. In exchange for not demanding that the guilty workers be fired, the supervisors could expect cooperation from them in the future. The supervisors also created obligations with the union stewards who, under normal conditions, would be expected to defend their own men even if their men were guilty. The supervisors, by not reporting the thefts, could keep the union stewards from being put in that embarrassing position, thereby ensuring industrial peace and some supervisory control at the expense of some of the company's merchandise. In this example, the thefts represent a symptom of a more basic problem: the inadvertent undercutting of the authority of the lower level supervisors when union-management contracts are negotiated by only top officials. If supervisors feel that if they act responsibly and try to control theft it would only mean that top management would not support them, then why be responsible to a top management that appears not to care about *their* work situation? Loyalty and responsibility can never be taken for granted; they must be earned in the day-to-day operations in the company.

Feelings produced by conflicts in the work setting are seldom expressed by the workers as constructive suggestions made to superiors in an attempt to change things. Attempting to reason with the upper level managers is difficult, and in an atmosphere of mutual distrust, not likely to succeed anyway. Moreover, the most dissatisfied workers, knowing this, may complain the *least* about the problems of their job. But the problems do not vanish because they aren't expressed. The problems eventually show up in indirect ways. There are many such indirect symptoms of underlying organizational conflict, each of which potentially cuts into productivity, morale, and the quality of work life.

Many of these symptoms can be spotted by examining company records or just by listening to what people are saying on their coffee breaks or in the lunchroom. We will discuss three different types of symptoms of underlying conflict to look for, which can manifest themselves in many ways. An organization that is having problems may have all or just a few of these or similar symptoms. Some symptoms indicate that an avoidance of conflict in the job setting is occurring. Other symptoms indicate that conflicts are being repressed or, as we have expressed it in Chapter 1, "feelings are being swallowed." Finally, there are symptoms that indicate a reactive response to conflict. These are organizational symptoms connected to what in Chapter 1 we called the "attacker" response.

Symptoms of Underlying Conflict
  I. Avoidance of conflict
    1. Absenteeism
    2. Hiding out
    3. "Yessing" the boss
  II. Repressive responses to conflict
    4. Ill health
    5. Escapist drinking
    6. Low job satisfaction
    7. Irregular output
  III. Reactive responses to conflict
    8. Rumor mill
    9. Stealing and destruction
    10. Counterorganization
    11. Wildcat strikes

Avoidance of Conflict

ABSENTEEISM   When people like their work they come to work, but when there is a problem in the work setting, then almost any other activity they have to do in their lives becomes a reason for not going to work. When people find their jobs frustrating and unrewarding, they can always find excuses for not showing up. There are, of course, many reasons for missing a day of work now and then, and people do have crises in their personal lives which sometimes cause them to miss work. Normally we would expect these kinds of personal problems to be evenly distributed among the employees of a company. When we notice that certain sections of a company have much higher rates of absenteeism than others, then absenteeism is a tip-off that tells you that there is a basic problem in the work situation of that section.

HIDING OUT   Some people are never at their desks or at their stations, but are off in some other part of the company delivering a message or checking on some item. This may be a symptom that reflects these individuals' basic desire to be somewhere else. The fact that you can never find these people may indicate that they are trying to avoid a conflict situation.

"YESSING" THE BOSS   When the staff agrees privately among themselves that the boss should face up to a distressing problem but no one is willing to bring up the problem, or when the boss and his or her staff agree too rapidly on a problem and its solution, then the employees are considered to be "yessing" the boss. When relationships between individuals are good, people are able to face distressing issues and examine critically the different alternatives to a problem, but when relationships between individuals are tense and strained, then avoiding distressing problems or jumping to a quick consensus is a way of avoiding open conflict. In such a situation avoidance undermines the basic decision-making process within the company, with predictably bad consequences for the quality of the decisions and the effectiveness of their implementation.

Repressive Responses to Conflict

ILL HEALTH   When people have headaches, don't feel good, or suffer fatigue, it may be that they are actually ill, but it may be that they are "sick of work." It has become common knowledge in industrial relations that when people are denied social support, their jobs become more stressful and they begin to suffer symptoms of ill health. By simply examining who is taking the most aspirin or stomach medication in your company, you may be able to identify areas of organizational stress and conflict.

ESCAPIST DRINKING   The fact that people drink a few beers, a glass of wine, or a martini does not indicate that their work situation is bothering them. It is a different matter when people drink to relax from the pressures of their job or to forget about their job. Escapist drinking is not necessarily alcoholism, nor does it necessarily involve drinking on the job. But it does involve the job: If the job situation were less stressful and more rewarding, employees would be less concerned about forgetting it. Escapist drinking as a pattern of social life thus may be a symptom of underlying organizational conflict. Some organizational consulting firms work with a questionnaire that is devoted almost entirely to health habits—drinking, exercise, sleep, and so forth—based on this insight.

LOW JOB SATISFACTION   You do not need to give people a paper-and-pencil questionnaire to find out that they are not satisfied with their jobs; most of the time they will simply tell you. They may simply say that their work is not as interesting as it used to be or that they are not as motivated as they once were. When people are telling you that they intend to leave their job and find a better one but they never seem to really look for another job, then they are expressing low job satisfaction without actually knowing why they are unhappy. All of these things point to low job satisfaction, and low job satisfaction is one of the best indications of basic conflicts and stresses in the job situation.

IRREGULAR OUTPUT   When similar or comparable parts of a company vary greatly in the amount or the quality of their production, this is an indication that something is basically wrong in one of the areas. When different parts of the company vary a great deal in social events, for example, in acknowledging birthdays or having Christmas parties each year, then you might want to investigate other aspects of social relations in the problem units. The indications are hard to describe, but they are often easily noticed. Do people appear friendly or hostile? Trusting or suspicious? Do they show concern for others, or do you get the sense that they just don't care? Do they just do the job and leave it at that? Are they unproductive and sloppy in their work output? If many of these things are true, you have a basic underlying conflict situation.

Reactive Responses to Conflict

RUMOR MILL   When rumors sweep through the company about firings, conflicts, layoffs, or shutdowns, people are responding to more than just the new information. A company's rumors, whether true or false, tell you the kinds of things people are ready to uncritically believe. If the employees of a company are ready to uncritically believe bad news, then that is because they unconsciously expect only bad news. This is a symptom of stress and conflict in the organization.

STEALING AND DESTRUCTION   When companies have a rash of stealing, destructiveness, and sabotage, it is often a good indication that the problem goes beyond simply having one troublesome individual, particularly when several individuals in a unit of a company may be involved. Generally, we can say that people don't steal from other people in organizations of which they feel a part. Stealing, destruction, and sabotage are often a symptom of the "who cares?" attitude. When employees feel that the company doesn't care about them and that they are easily expendable, then some of the employees may let the company know that they don't think much of the company, either. Rashes of stealing, destructiveness, and sabotage may represent reactive responses to frustrations and stresses found in the general working atmosphere of the company.

COUNTERORGANIZATION   When a company experiences rapid and easy union organization and the establishment of a collective bargaining unit, it usually represents a long-term buildup of frustrations and grievances among the employees. Normally, union organization in a company is not a rapid and spontaneous process. There is considerable reluctance on the part of the workers to organize unless most of them are fed up and do not believe that they have any chance of being treated fairly. Not every section of the company will be equally enthusiastic about the creation of a union and collective bargaining unit; therefore, some of the conflict relationships can be identified by looking at which sections and which workers within the company push the hardest for the formation of a union. Whether the union wins a collective bargaining election or not, companies should identify and eliminate those basic frustrations and conflicts to restore cooperation and productivity within the company.

WILDCAT STRIKES   The orderly relation between a company and the union is represented in the basic contract, but when workers feel that the company is not treating them fairly and that their union is not dealing with the real problems of their work in the contract negotiation, frustration begins to build up, and a wildcat strike may occur. These strikes generally are set off by a particular incident to which workers attach a symbolic significance. Yet the wildcat strike may not tell us very much about what is actually wrong in the work situation. The particular issue may seem trivial. The strike happens because the workers feel that nobody is paying attention to their needs.

You should remember that wildcat strikes represent not only a grievance against the company but also a grievance against the union. The underlying conflict situations are especially difficult and complex to analyze and find solutions for, for they involve the organizational problems of the union as well as of the company. Often managers are gleeful about conflicts in the union, on the principle that it means "confusion to the enemy." This is a self-destructive mistake in most cases—the company is likely to suffer from the conflicts as much as will the union. The workers who distrust the union will likely distrust the management even more. When managers attempt to exploit the situation, there is likely to be a backlash.

The symptoms do not identify the disease. Each symptom or combination of them may represent a simple underlying problem or a very complex one that will take time and resources to correct. Identifying the symptoms only represents a preliminary step.

CONCLUSION

In this chapter we have indicated some of the hidden consequences of conflict relationships by focusing attention on the coping behavior of individuals in an organization. These coping behaviors are the symptoms of underlying problems. Yet they are often difficult to recognize as methods of coping. Individuals can always give reasons for their behavior. They can say that they are too busy, that they are tied up with other matters, or that they have a headache that day. These are all legitimate excuses for not doing the tasks that either would bring them into conflict with other people in the organization or would force the basic problem out into the open. For the most part, an organization can contrive effective strategies to hide basic conflict relationships, but it usually can't avoid showing some symptoms of these underlying conflicts. Finding these symptoms of underlying conflicts tells us that the problems are there, but it does not tell us what the problems are or how to solve them. Solving the problems by eliminating the symptoms may be as ineffective as trying to cure measles with a skin cream.

4

HOT SPOTS,
PRESSURE POINTS,
AND THE STRUCTURE
OF SITUATIONS

In the examples we've discussed so far, we've been faced with the problem of rethinking situations, and rethinking them in a particular way. We've begun in each case with an everyday way of thinking about the whys and wherefores of what people do and ought to do, and have used an ordinary, everyday vocabulary to characterize their motives, personalities, opinions, and attitudes toward themselves and others on the job. We've then looked at the situations all over again and described them using a different, organizational, or "situational," vocabulary. We might call this a process of rereading the situation.

This process of rereading is what organizational analysis is all about. In this chapter we will look at the process, and we will introduce, in a much more systematic way, some rules for reading conflict situations. "Rules," however, is much too formal a term for what will be given, as we shall see, so perhaps we should say that we will provide some materials that will enable you to reanalyze the situation and make a "new reading."

All of this sounds mysterious, so let's consider some other examples of "rereadings" that managers use. Consider a PERT diagram or some similar work flow diagram. To write one up, you take the tasks you need performed in order to complete a job and then arrange them on a page, according to particular rules for the use of time and steps involved in each task. A common way of going about this is to write the tasks on stickers, and then stick each task to a page or sheet, which has been arranged with a time line running down the bottom, so that the spaces between the places one sticks the tasks represents the maximum necessary amount of time that each job can be expected to take. By working backwards, one can learn how long the total job will take. By arranging each task that needs to be done before another task is done on a sequential line, one can learn when any series of tasks needs to be started in order to get the total project done on time.

What we are doing here is reordering (rereading and rethinking) the tasks according to particular rules—none too rigid—of what to include as tasks and how to arrange them. The personalities of employees, costs, personnel training, and a great many other factors in the process of getting the job done drop out. For this moment at least, we rethink the situation in a certain way, describe the tasks as tasks, order them according to the order of time sequences, and follow the system of putting stickers, with one task on each, on a sheet of paper in series, arranged backwards from the completion of the task. Thus, by oversimplifying the actual work process we can get a better picture of how we need to plan.

So the purpose of a PERT diagram is clear: It enables us to plan. The purpose of rethinking that one does in connection with time-motion studies, or any other kind of decision structure, is that of increasing efficiency. With organizational conflict, we also have a clear purpose: Identify the problem in a way that enables us to act to deal with the conflict. Simplifying, redescribing, and reordering can also be used to reduce conflict. In a conflict situation, the materials and rules for the construction of the new reading or description of the situation are different than in a planning situation, and they serve a different purpose.

To analyze the problems of organizational conflict, we need a set of rules, or guides, that will tell us what facts to pick out and how to arrange them. Where do we get such a list? The obvious source is the large literature on organizations and management theory that has developed since the rise of "scientific management" at the end of the nineteenth century. None of the theories or perspectives that have been developed in the subsequent discussion of the problems of management has solved the problems, and there are no ideal patterns for organizational life. Indeed, the glaring inadequacies of each new announced model of organization suggest that there may be something wrong with the idea of a perfect "theory of organization." However, each wave of theory has given us a few useful ideas and information, or has served to point out some important, neglected feature of organizational life that is relevant to conflict.

STEP ONE ANALYSIS: HOT SPOTS AND PRESSURE POINTS

In Chapter 2 we saw that conflict usually involves either a situation in which there is a relationship where friction occurs or an individual who is unable to cope with conflicting pressures and demands. The troublesome relationships we will call "pressure points." The troublesome situations we will call "hot spots." We will use these ideas as first steps, or ordering principles, which we will later show how to reread or rethink.

Pressure Points

The places where the fights start, the feelings get bruised, and the blame gets directed are known as pressure points. In the example of the word processing center discussed in the last chapter, the pressure point was the relationship between the teachers, who wanted the projectors, and the word processing employees, whose work was interrupted by the job of pushing the projectors around. In a restaurant, a major pressure point forms between the waiters or order takers and the cooks. In a repair business, the pressure point can be between the sales clerks and the repair people. You can usually tell where a pressure point exists because when people tell their stories about what's wrong they tend to personalize the problem; they may characterize the person at the other side of the pressure point as inconsiderate, demanding, inaccurate, and otherwise "difficult." The difficulties people describe in these stories are talked about as if they were "not part of the job."

In a restaurant, dealing with difficult customers is part of the waiter's job, one of the taken-for-granted features of the waiter's role. Waiters find ways of coping with difficult or demanding customers, often by completely dehumanizing them to minimize their effect on the work situation. Thus, customers aren't a source of "conflict." When the onrush of customers increases the pace of work during the lunch hour, and waiters are demanding that the kitchen provide food in a rush, then friction with the cooks *is* a source of conflict, because that friction is not "part of the job." The job requires the cooperation of the waiter and the cook; without this cooperation the job becomes impossible. If the cook gets angry and refuses to prepare new batches of food so that the waiter must tell the customer that the restaurant is out of an item, or if the cook refuses to be pushed, then the waiter is caught in the middle between hungry customers and angry cooks. Here we have a pressure point. In such a situation there is no time for soothing hurt feelings, and the expectation is still one of cooperation, even though conflict results. There is an important lesson in this example. By establishing a routine, through the use of an order spindle, the cooks can fill one order at a time, and the waiters can see how long it may be before their orders are filled. This reduces the friction-causing interaction between the cooks and the waiters, and it removes much of the conflict by redefining part of the job.

Why can such a simple device have such happy results? The main reason is that it changes the nature of the social relation between the waiters and the cook. In the old system, in which the waiters gave the cooks verbal orders, there were some serious sources of friction. One had to do with status. The cooks, who think of themselves as superior to the waiters in importance and prestige, had to take orders from the waiters as though they were their flunkies. To show the waiters who were really the bosses, the cooks could easily "block" by slowing up the orders. Another source of friction resulted from the fact that verbal orders vanished into the air and couldn't be checked. Consequently, when there was a disagreement over what had been said, there was no way to resolve it, and each side accused the other of making a mistake or purposely screwing up. Naturally, accusations led to resentment.

The new system can give the cooks a sense of control. Rather than being the waiters' flunkies, harassed by orders, the cooks can be in charge of the task of dealing with orders most efficiently. Slips of paper seem less like "taking orders" in our culture than like receiving requests. The status issue thus becomes less of an irritant and, finally, the issues over mistakes are depersonalized. No one needs to make accusations or suspect that the other is trying to screw him or her up. They can all refer to that impersonal slip of paper. The person who makes the mistake can then be found out. This is an inducement not to make mistakes in the future, as well as an inducement not to create too much ado over someone else's mistakes, because anyone's mistakes, under this system—including one's own—can be found out.

Hot Spots

These are the jobs that people quit as soon as they can, or in which they turn sour, become double-dealers, or act erratically. Sociologists use the term *role conflict* to describe the situation that applies to many of these jobs. Role conflicts happen when two or more sets of expectations, many of which can't be met, are placed on the occupant of the same position. To cope with these jobs, the occupant double-deals, puts people off, manipulates, tries to compromise, or chooses one set of expectations to fulfill. In doing this, the job is usually not blamed, the people are. Some of the people who deal with the person in the hot spot are likely to experience these relations as a pressure point, and the employee in the role conflict position, in dealing with the people in other positions in the organization, is likely to experience some of them as pressure points. So the *people*, not the jobs, will be blamed for the troubles.

STEP TWO ANALYSIS: IDENTIFYING DEEPER CONFLICT CAUSES

As we have seen, clues to understanding conflict are the ways in which the ordinary vocabulary of blame and fault are used. Conflicts are situations in which people disagree about who is at fault. The aim of rethinking, or rereading, a conflict situation is to look at the structure in such a way that blame no longer becomes the focus.

The first thing one must forget in this rethinking is the question of "who is really at fault." Fault, or at least the disagreement about fault, becomes the thing that is to be written out of the analysis. We are looking for a way to talk about the situation in which there is no person at fault, or in which there are no "two sides" to the story.

We should read the situation in the structure, not in the people. The structure is the whole arrangement of work and social relations, and not just the relations defined by an organization chart. Yet the organization chart is analogous to the structure in an important sense. The chart depicts relationships that are true regardless of *who* is in each position: Relations are between offices or jobs and not between real people with personalities and individual styles. Similarly, the structure, as we need to think of it, is something that holds regardless of who is in any given position. However, the kinds of relationships included in the notion of structure are broader. Among relationships, for example, are those in which a person checks out his or her standards of "good work" and his or her sense of "doing a job properly." These relationships are an extremely important source of worth for people, and also, as we will see in the next chapter, a common element in conflict.

These other relations are important, and we will discuss them at length. But the easiest starting point in understanding the structure is the visible tip of the iceberg, namely, the official written rules governing jobs and authority, such as job descriptions and the organization chart.

The Chart

According to the organization chart, who is whose boss? What is the chain of command? Who gives orders, and to whom are they given? Who is responsible for what kind of problems? Some organizations are more obsessed with these questions than are others. Governments generally have elaborate organization charts; small businesses have less elaborate charts or no charts at all. For some organizations, there are few written rules. In many organizations, the written rules aren't even known to most of the participants.

Job Descriptions

What applies for organization charts applies for formal job descriptions. Some organizations are obsessed by them. In other organizations, one might have to look up one's own job description to find out what it says and doesn't say. Many job descriptions are open-ended, ending with such phrases as "and other duties as required."

Both the rules and the job descriptions, then, tell you only a part of how the job is actually done. Even in organizations where there is an obsession with the rules and with job descriptions, the rules and the job descriptions don't tell you everything about job performance. There is also an "informal structure," or an unwritten daily expectation of people in the work situation, which gives us more of the materials or elements we need to do a job and use as part of our rethinking of a conflict situation. The informal structure contains various elements that are not as neatly packaged as are rules and job descriptions.

Communication

In a given job, who does one go to when he or she needs to find out how to get something done? Who does one go to in order to send up a signal to a supervisor or higher-up without confronting that person directly? People avoid face-to-face confrontations when they can. This applies even more to encounters with higher-ups! Employees who get instructions from their bosses that they don't understand or don't know how to carry out rarely go back to the bosses and ask for a clarification. They usually go to those on their own level for some advice. Of course, if you are a manager or supervisor, the same phenomenon is seen, both in your relations with *your* higher-ups and in your relations with your subordinates. When you give an order, your subordinate has to interpret it. He or she probably won't come to you for help, but will go to certain other people who can be asked without risk. Thus, to fully understand the job structure, you need to know who a given person turns to when he or she has a question or needs advice.

The patterns here can be very interesting. Some "units" are competitive and involve a high level of mutual suspicion and distrust. In a competitive sales staff, for example, the other salespeople might not be the people to whom one could turn. As an observer you should notice what kind of relationships people have with one another. Find out whether people are intimate enough to associate after work, or whether they are merely intimate enough to joke with one another. A relationship that is not very intimate and that is perhaps edged with some hostility can exhibit some biting humor. You can tell, by observation, where a person is picking up ideas about such things as what the job is about, what is expected, and the folklore associated with a particular job. These relationships are where a person gets ideas about how well he or she is doing and what is really expected of him or her.

An old lesson taught by management theory is that "a worker wishes first and foremost to have the esteem of his fellows." This may be somewhat overstated, and it is often not completely clear what counts as "esteem" for a certain person or who his "fellows" are. But the slogan points to a fact that we can use. A person's sources and points of reference are as much part of the job as are the rules and job description, and they can be elements in the conflict situation.

Doing the Job

People strive to make a job into a meaningful activity, and they assign standards of adequacy or good practice to their work. One of the things that those studying scientific management discovered right away was that the job habits of the workers were often not the best for the entire organization. When managers used time-and-motion studies to rethink their jobs, workers adjusted very painfully and unhappily, although in many cases the jobs were made less injurious and the pay was increased. Why should this have been so? One reason, though not the only one, was that the worker's own way of doing the job was something in which he or she took pride—it was part of the worker's sense of doing the job properly, on the one hand, and, on the other, something with which the worker identified personally as a part of a well-done task. Consider the legend of John Henry, who worked on the construction of the railroads by driving spikes by hand. When the steam hammer was introduced, he challenged it to a contest to prove his superiority to the machine. This legend celebrates John Henry's sense of pride in his skill or prowess in doing a job well. Of course, we sympathize with John Henry, although we know that it would hardly be rational to trade in our technology for the backbreaking work of driving spikes by hand.

Once better ways of mowing were invented, we stopped cutting the grass with manual mowers, because hand lawnmowing was not our life's work, identity, and source of self-esteem, unlike John Henry's spike-driving. In our jobs, we cling to the things that are to us, as John Henry's hammer was to him, a lifework and a source of self-esteem and identity, and that are central to our sense of good practice, craftsmanship, and of a job well done. On one level, this is a source of resistance to change, but on another level, it is the core of work, the core of commitment to the tasks that are the work of the organization. No amount of managerial mumbo-jumbo about motivation, authority, leadership, or human relations is going to get as much work done well as will this commitment. Therefore, whatever changes we make, we should be very cautious about this one. If we try to "build trust" or "exercise authority," we need to think of this core as a force that can be used for or against the organization.

In many (if not most) conflict situations, people think that someone else is keeping them from doing their job well. In one sense, a conflict situation is one in which this basic force that runs the work of the organization is turned against itself. In the next chapter, when we talk about redoing or rewriting the organization in ways that don't produce a particular conflict, we will be seeing how to channel this force productively.

Evaluation and Pay Structure

The two areas that look disarmingly simple about an organization are in the pay structure and the system of evaluating employees. The reason they look simple is that there are tangible documents—paychecks and evaluation forms—that give the processes an objective look. Yet these two areas of an organization can produce more hurt feelings and bitterness than any other areas in the operation of an organization. Everyone knows that there is more to these areas than the simple assignment of ratings and granting of pay raises. Employees usually feel that some people earn their pay and others don't and that some evaluations are meaningful and others aren't. Herein lies the difficulty, because the meaning and value that an employee places on a piece of paper may be sharply different than that of the manager. A formal system of evaluation or pay creates a pattern of comparisons that may conform to or contrast with the pattern of "deep structure" social comparisons that emerge out of the daily working relationships within the organization.

Let us consider this with evaluations. A supervisor knows that subordinates may react to a bad critical evaluation by taking revenge, by not putting out work, or by sabotaging the supervisor by causing delays. On the other hand, a supervisor can create problems for an employee by giving her or him too positive an evaluation, which would be interpreted by others as undeserved praise. This can give the employee the reputation of being a "brown-noser" in the eyes of his fellow workers. If it is difficult to fire people or difficult to fill their positions, the supervisor is severely constrained to evaluate the employees in a way that does not anger them or appear unjust. At the same time, subordinates know that there is slack in any system, even in a performance appraisal or task-oriented type of evaluation, and that you need to do things that aren't in the job description to keep the boss happy. Many of these things you might do unconsciously, such as keeping a cheerful look on your face or not confronting the boss with a problem you know he does not like to deal with.

Normally we might feel that the evaluation mechanism is an instrument of defining expectations on both sides. In the hands of the evaluator, it is a means of enforcing expectations; for the employees, it is a crystal ball in which some of the true expectations of the boss can be glimpsed. We should, however, see the evaluation mechanism as an entire system of expectations. The boss is not the only one to set expectations—the employees have their own expectations for how they should do their job and how others should do their jobs and what constitutes a good or bad performance. If we ignore the fact that employees have their own ideas of how they are doing and how others are doing, we will never understand why a system of evaluation can cause conflict. If in the daily work performance a boss asks too much or does not follow through on efforts to live up to expectations by rewarding the employee with a good performance evaluation, then the "community of expectations" is destroyed and the boss and the employees may start to "teach the other a lesson" or force the other to "shape up."

Pay levels, like evaluations, pass signals—and sometimes the wrong signals—from bosses to employees. These signals often cause serious difficulties in an organization, as we shall see. Let's start from the point of view that presumes that everyone wants more money; then let's ask the question, *What is the worth of money to an employee?* It sounds like a silly question because salary size is associated with how comfortable one's lifestyle is, but are there other values that a salary or a pay raise can represent for the employee? If we can narrow down some of the additional values and expectations that are associated with a level of pay in an organization, then we can isolate some of the factors that can lead to the conflict caused by indiscriminate pay raises. Because money has a specific value for the employee and for the organization and because levels of pay differentiate among employees in an exact way, the pay structure of an organization can become the focal point for internal conflicts.

Let's use as an illustration some of the feelings and expectations of an employee who gets a 10 percent raise. First, her base rate of pay is taken to represent the firm's idea of the worth of that worker, and a 10 percent pay raise may represent an increase in the relative worth of the worker or it may represent in the eyes of the worker a relative decline in her worth. If everyone in the company has gotten a 10 percent raise and the employee considered here is a low-paid worker, then she remains a low-paid worker plus 10 percent; the fact that people spend dollars, not percentages, means that her raise represents fewer dollars than the top executives' raises, even though the percentages have been the same. If, however, this worker gets a 10 percent raise and the people whose base salary is higher than hers get a 3 percent raise, then her raise represents a relative increase in her worth to the company. On the other hand, if highly paid employees in the company get a 15 percent raise and she only gets a 10 percent raise, she may regard her raise as an insult and an affront to her worth as an employee. The point here is that the worth of money to the employee is a relative worth based on certain kinds of comparisons that might be made with people in other job categories.

The employee may also make her evaluation about her raise in terms of a set of comparisons between her fellow workers who do roughly the same job as she does. In this case, she may feel that she deserves more than Mr. Jones who gets the same 10 percent raise, because she feels she works harder and does a better job than Mr. Jones. If, on the other hand, she gets a higher raise in dollars or in percentage than Mr. Jones, she may not only feel she is being rewarded for her hard work, but she may feel reassured that her job is not superfluous. In this case, the employee's feelings of increased worth become related to feelings of job security. When employees' pay expectations are met, they usually become more willing to accept difficulties and pressures in their jobs, because they feel that this is what they are paid for. When the employees' relative pay expectations are not met, they may feel that some of the demands of their jobs are things that are not warranted, so they feel that they are not being paid to put up with such demands.

The question is, *How can we make sense out of the kinds of social comparisons that employees make to determine whether their rate of pay or their salary raise is adequate?* The answer lies in identifying and isolating "distribution rules." The distribution rules determine whether a particular pay reference is appropriate for evaluating an employee's level of pay. These distribution rules may never be written down or openly quoted; nevertheless, they represent certain agreed-upon standards of equity and fairness. For example, a simple distribution rule may be "people performing similar work shall receive similar pay," or another simple distribution rule may be "people with similar training, education, or experience shall get similar pay." We might expect that by analyzing the distribution rules we could anticipate conflict if people who had the same amount of education and training got different rates of pay or if people with different levels of education and training got the same rate of pay.

There is usually a high degree of tacit agreement that there should be a justice to the relative pay level, and so inequities cause workers to want to "even things up." If the company or the top executives are the ones who are blamed for these inequities, the evening up may take the form of slacking off work, pilferage, or destruction of equipment. If intermediate supervisors are blamed, employees may be less cooperative or may simply slow down work in ways that make the supervisor look bad. If fellow employees are seen as causing the inequities in the system, then they may be isolated as being unethical "brown-nosers." Often the method of evening things up available to the employee is not the one that attacks the true source of the problem. Resentment, which is an extraordinarily large part of organizational conflict situations, is like a loose force that can fasten onto any element of the problematic situation. Whether it is related to the structural problem or not, it takes a certain amount of patience and skill to trace a problem back to its structural underpinnings in the system of evaluation and pay.

Respect and Status Structure

"I don't get no respect" is more than a comic's line. In organizations, it is one of the main ways in which resentment is formulated, and therefore is a crucial trouble signal. To think this through, we must consider some of the places in organizations where people do "get respect," apart from the sort of "respect" you might get simply as a result of being in a position of power or a "position of respect."

The primary example of this latter type of respect is that which is given to professionals or to people who can claim a special right to run their jobs as they see fit—within some limits. To be sure, not all professionals feel that they get enough respect. Nevertheless, the claim that occupations make to being "professions" is motivated in large part by the realization that respect and autonomy, or freedom to run a job as one's trained judgment tells one, is a great bulwark against those demands made by the organization. "Professionaliza- tion" of an occupation is often the practitioner's demand to forma- lize the autonomy needed to live up to his or her sense of what the job is supposed to entail. Respect is connected to this in this way: Respect is a sort of honoring of limits (for example, think of what "respectable girls" *do* and what *isn't done* to them).

As with evaluations and pay, people like to even things up when they don't feel they get enough respect. As with blame, the way people think about what would be enough respect, and who should give it, rarely corresponds to the way people in other organizational positions think. Ordinarily, this diversity of ideas isn't an open prob- lem in the organization. Respect, after all, is a matter of what people give without being asked or coerced. If you have to ask for respect, whatever it is you get back isn't going to be respect, but, at best, some reassuring words. People sometimes turn these words into suffi- cient evidence of respect in their own minds for their own purposes.

Indeed, many things can be treated as signs of respect, so in looking at problems of respect in an organization, we are looking at an exchange of token actions, from responses such as, "Who does he think he is to ask me to do that!" and "We know you are the best graphic designer in the company, so. . . " The thing to notice about these exchanges is that the value of what is said does not correspond in any direct way to the value of what is done in return. Like the Indians who sold Manhattan for some blankets and trinkets, people in organizations often sell their careers for a compliment or some other modest mark of respect or status.

An organization breaks down when people feel that a serious imbalance exists between status or the signs of respect given to them and what they deserve. A good slogan that often fits people's be- havior is: They can't get justice, so they settle for vengeance. This phrase was used recently to describe the reaction of the police in a troubled police department to the killing of a police officer. The way they got "justice" was to go out and kill a person innocent of that crime, on the principle "If one of us dies, one of them has to die." If people in your organization don't think they are getting justice, they can find many ways of evening things up, thereby *making* a rough form of the justice that they don't freely get. Again, the way they make this rough justice depends not on some abstract truth about what's really happening in the organization, but on the materials they have at hand. If the material they have at hand is an innocent person to blame and criticize, they will.

This backbiting and criticism is often the way that an organizational problem surfaces, yet it is most mysterious to a manager, for it seems so irrational and misdirected, and so easy to regard as a personality problem on the part of the person doing the criticizing. Worse, it usually leads the manager in the wrong direction. The manager's first impulse is often to punish the person doing the criticizing. What the act or criticism really signals, however, is that this person feels an imbalance, and feels that a balance needs to be restored among the workers.

WORKSHEETS

There are three worksheets for this chapter, preceded by an observation sheet. You will find them in the appendix. The work relationships observation sheet will help you uncover the informal job structure and will signal a problem that needs to be explored further. The worksheets, the pressure point sheet, and the two structure sheets are meant to be used as guides to rethinking a conflict situation. Start with sheet one, the pressure point sheet. Make copies of the sheet so you can fill one out for each individual who is involved in the conflict. For each employee, fill out the sheet on the basis of the behavior that you have observed. If you haven't noticed these behaviors or feelings yet, make it your business to keep an eye out for more information.

If you are the supervisor, you can also "go public" with the sheets, that is, use the sheets as a guide to asking questions about the conflict situation in interviews with the people in the situation and tell them that you are asking the same questions of everyone. You may find out a few things about yourself as a manager by comparing your preinterview impressions to the things you are told in the interviews! Interviews alone, however, are never enough. People "stage manage" their face-to-face contacts, just as you are putting on a performance for your employees and bosses. So you need to keep your ears open for things other than the things that are said, and evaluate the things that are said by considering their meaning in light of what you can observe for yourself. The pressure point sheet, then, is a guide to what to *look* and *listen* for, not just what to ask.

The second and third sheets, the structure sheets, are where the basic work of rereading the situation is done. When you first look at an organizational conflict, you see personalities. These sheets are your means of reading the situation in a new way, with the personalities left out. The sheets are a list of the facts in the organization that make up the structure, including both the formal and informal structure. The sections in this chapter explain the things you need to notice and write on the sheets.

This two-step rethinking of the organization is the basis for reconstructing the situation in a way that eliminates the conflicts. *How* to eliminate them is the subject of the next chapter.

5

REDOING THE SETUP

So far we've been discussing the elements of conflict that cause problems relating to work distribution, prestige, and with whom people check out their attitudes. In this chapter we are going to talk about how to rearrange these elements so that the conflicts are eliminated.

The most difficult part of thinking about these rearrangements, for most managers, is to get in the right frame of mind. In a conflict situation we are tempted to get emotionally involved and to focus on individuals; yet, as managers, we try not to get emotionally involved; so we feel we will be more objective if we think like judges—deciding who is right, who is wrong, and who deserves some form of punishment. Our verdicts are usually wrapped up with other verdicts we make, particularly verdicts about who really turns out the work in a unit, or who is a "key" employee and who is not.

Making these judgments is absolutely central to being a good manager. If you can't make them, or won't make them, you can't get the work done properly, and you will misuse your human resources and create organizational conflicts.

The problem with making these judgments is that the "judge" model is exactly the wrong model for thinking about rearranging an organization. To be sure, you need to have *already made* the right judgments about such things as who does the work and who doesn't, but the task of thinking up a rearrangement isn't a task of getting the rights and wrongs sorted out, and then rewarding the good and punishing the wicked. We need an entirely different frame of mind. The rights and wrongs of the past must be treated as a consequence of the way situations were set up. We have to think that the person who does a bad job isn't the problem; the job, and the way it's set up is the problem. Whether a person does a good job or not is a matter of the job, not the person.

Of course, sometimes this way of thinking about a situation—"thinking organizationally," let's call it—isn't the right way. Sometimes the problem *is* the person, and sometimes it's both the person and the situation, or it can be a little bit of both. Think of it this way. At one extreme there are *jobs* that nobody could do or be happy doing. There, and only there, do we have a pure "job" problem. At another extreme, there are *people* who can't do any job satisfactorily or happily. Between these extremes lie the bulk of the cases. However, we have to think about jobs and about people in two different ways, so we have to shift perspectives to begin to see the problems. Because most of the situations we deal with as managers are between the extremes, the ability to think both ways becomes a basic management skill.

In this chapter we will codify the "organizational thinking" skill—though not completely, since it is a skill, and not merely a technique. You can think of the rules we lay down here as a collection of reminders about what a solution for a conflict problem should include.

STEP ONE SOLUTIONS: HOT SPOTS AND PRESSURE POINTS

Solving problems by rearranging an organization is like trying to fix a clock. The more taking apart you do, the more trouble you are likely to have getting it to work properly again. Therefore, it is a good idea to try the easy things first. The more drastic the solution, the more drastic are the problems that can be created.

With a clock, your problem may be no more than a tiny bit of dirt in the mechanism at some vital point. This is often precisely what happens in an organization. One irritating procedure, one place where everyone gets rubbed the wrong way, can cause problems that are much more serious than the actual cause itself would lead you to believe.

In the last chapter we discussed identifying the pressure points and hot spots. Once you have identified them it is easy to consider, as a first step, solutions that deal only with relieving the problem of pressure points and hot spots. Keep in mind that the pressure-point solutions are only a first step, and may not work in situations where the pressure points are not a significant part of the problem or where the pressure points are part of a larger problem that requires a more drastic solution.

These "first step" solutions fall into roughly three categories:

A. Routinizing and depersonalizing
B. Rerouting communications around pressure points
C. Changing contact task assignments

Routinizing and Depersonalizing

If you've ever been in a crowded bar and waited patiently to be served, you've probably heard some loudmouth bark, "Who do you have to know to get a drink around here?" At the drive-in window of your favorite fast food restaurant, you never have that problem. Then again, you've never developed particularly warm feelings of loyalty, obligation, or comfortableness with the drive-in window attendant, as you might with a bartender. In work settings, the same dilemma exists. But when the intimacy of a work relationship *becomes* the source of trouble, depersonalizing it is a solution.

In Chapter 4 we discussed the classic example of depersonalization and routinization—the order wheel in a restaurant. The lesson to be learned from this is that a routine that can be checked by both parties involved reduces emotional friction by redirecting blame. The same lesson applies in many other circumstances and to many other techniques and procedures. When you go into a bakery, you take a number, because if there were no system for serving customers in

order, people would become irritated and feel that they had been unfairly treated. Without the system, they would blame the bakery
workers—with the system, they only have themselves to blame, because it is their fault that they didn't take a number or arrive early
enough to get a low number.

Bakeries and restaurants present relatively simple cases, but the
same lessons apply in complicated situations. If it is necessary to
make complicated priority judgments about what tasks are to be performed first, it is important to make sure that people feel that the
judgments are fair, and not being made on the basis of favoritism. By
constructing a system that can be checked or monitored by the people involved so that everyone knows or can determine that the system is being followed, any frustration or resentment can be directed
away from the people involved.

Drawbacks

The drawbacks to solutions like the number-taking routine are
often considerable. It's one thing to take a number in a crowded
bakery so that you know you'll be served in sequence. It's another
thing to follow that same rule in an empty bakery. "Procedures" are
always hassles, especially when they involve paperwork. And they
can be costly and time-consuming, as well as irritating. The cases
where they work best are when no *additional* paperwork results, such
as the order wheel solution, where the paper that has the order on it
is also the bill (and inventory control), or where the paperwork or
procedure creates something useful for both parties.

The following is a simple example of creating something useful
for both parties. Recall the example of the word processor operators
in the junior college who had to take charge of the audiovisual equipment. A common method of dealing with equipment requests is to
phone in reservations. However, this is disruptive, especially if it is
not the primary job of the request-taker to do this. Worse, this person suffers the burden of the paperwork and gets blamed for mistakes. Because of this, it's common to set up a procedure in which
the paperwork originates with the user, such as in the case of request
forms; it results in more hassle, but more precision, and more clarity
about responsibility for mistakes. But the problems with this can be
endless. All paperwork can go wrong by having omitted information,
mistakes in reading, mistakes in transferring information from one
piece of paper to another, and so on. These don't happen if there is a

verbal exchange with someone who knows exactly what to ask and who can read back what has been written down. If printed forms are used to minimize these problems, there are constant problems with the forms—new forms, old forms, no forms at the right places, forms that ask for too much or too little, and so on.

Guidelines

If we think of solutions that give advantages to both parties in the word processing situation, we can come up with something better. One advantage for the user would be an assurance that the equipment will be there when it's needed. If the procedure doubles as a reservation, that's an advantage. It might also serve as a self-reminder, helping the user remember to bring appropriate materials. A sheet or board with all the available equipment listed by type, time, and date, which could be initialed, might serve the purpose best. If it is put in an accessible place, where the users pass frequently, it's likely to work. But the more hassles involved, and the smaller the advantage, the less likely it is to work. When you have to send out memos reminding or ordering people to use the procedure, it's a good bet that the procedure is failing. Don't lean on your authority; figure out what's wrong, and try to adjust the incentives accordingly. You might make people who don't use the procedure fetch their own equipment, for example, but don't expect anyone to put up with an additional hassle as a *favor* to you or to anyone else. All the training, all the memos, and all the meetings in the world won't make *that* work. Remember, what may seem to you like an innocuous request may seem like a major burden to the person you are asking. Most jobs use too many forms now. Any new one had better have a good justification. One final note. Nowadays in many organizations the job of the secretary is mostly taken up by filling out forms. So keep this in mind when you make up a new form or procedure: The person who agrees to use the form may not be the one who will do the work or have the problems with it, so get the support of the secretaries, who are the real users.

Rerouting around Pressure Points

When pressure points also involve status or authority problems, often the easiest solution is to pass the requests, memos, or orders indirectly through the superiors of the people doing the work. This method has the dual advantage of allowing the superior to keep tabs on what is being done and provides the subordinate with a clear sense of authority. There can be big problems with doing this, however, as we will see shortly.

The usual situation in which rerouting is an appropriate solution is where requests, work orders, messages, or planning decisions need to be passed between work units. As an example, let's consider the engineering unit of a factory, which needs to be notified if something is going wrong in a particular process, so that the machines can be fixed, adjusted, or replaced. The simplest way to make these arrangements would seem to be that as soon as the process starts going wrong, the engineering unit should be sent a message and the work should get started. But what seems to be simple is too simple here. Does the lowest level machine operator decide when the process is going wrong? Does this employee drop his work and run off to the engineering unit?

In the best of all possible worlds, the engineers would be working on something that could be interrupted, could instantly understand the problem from the description given by the machine operator, and could promptly go and fix things. In the real world, the decision as to whether anything is actually going wrong may be very difficult; the engineers—who don't like the idea of "taking orders" from the machine operator—may not be able to learn what the problem is from what the machine operator says and may not believe or be interested in what the machine operator is telling them. In addition, the engineers may blame the machine operator for breaking the machinery or causing a malfunction, when in fact the machinery may simply need routine maintenance. The usual solution is to have someone with higher rank—the immediate supervisor or the area supervisor, for example—listen to the machine operator's problem and then relate the problem to the engineers. Sometimes this helps, but sometimes it doesn't, because the supervisors may not understand what is going wrong and may end up misdescribing the problem, which could lead to delays and confusion.

The costs of communication problems such as these can be enormous, so the issue is usually reduced to blame and responsibility. The engineer is in an especially powerful position for shifting the blame onto other people, however. The job of the engineer consists of highly technical work that can only be properly assessed by another engineer. Therefore, no one else can blame him for costly production delays and expect anyone to take the accusations seriously. The engineer can always find someone else to blame, or he can at least thoroughly confuse the issue.

Engineers are not the only ones whose expert knowledge gives them an advantage in disputes. Members of every profession, indeed those in every organizational occupation with "expert knowledge," have much the same advantage. One consequence of this is that conflicts often arise at the point where not everyone can say who is responsible.

One common reason for these problems is that the goals of the units—the engineering unit as opposed to the line production unit, for example—actually conflict in many situations. This becomes obvious when we look not at the "goals" that the engineering unit has on paper, but at what the unit and the people in the unit are actually rewarded and punished for. Often what one discovers when looking at the constraints is that by doing the ordinary things that the company needs done, the unit looks bad. If the unit needs more staff to take care of production problems, it will have to have a higher budget. The head of engineering may know that the company never really blames his unit for process problems on the line, but he knows he does get blamed for increasing his budget. The signals he gets from the situation are "don't ask" for more staff. So he concentrates on getting the "work" of the unit done—writing reports, advising about purchases of equipment, and so forth. His reasoning is, "We can't always be running down to the production line and holding their hands; anyway, if the line gets behind, that's their problem, at least they'll be the ones who will have to explain themselves. It's quite another thing for engineering to be late with a report to the front office. That's one thing that I have to take the heat on."

Drawbacks
The drawback to rerouting is that the people who pass on the messages, requests, or orders may have little interest in enforcing the requests. The only effect is simply to add another step to an already trouble-ridden process. The advantage of rerouting through the office of a superior is that presumably the superior has an interest in the job getting done. However, this isn't always a correct presumption. The task may have a low priority for the superior whose main concerns lie elsewhere. Also, the fact that the superior is "superior,"

which is the basis of the success of routing through the superior's office, also can work against the task. We previously talked about how moving responsibilities up the hierarchy of an organization often amounted to little more than making the people with the problems shut up; the risks in complaining to a higher-up are such that even when the complaint is well justified, it won't be made. Rather than risk the problems of dealing with higher-ups, people often try to cope with the problems themselves, and this is often costly to the organization.

Changing Contact Task Assignments

Sometimes the pressure point is a result of a lack of certain personal skills that are irrelevant to the primary job task. A mechanic can be a first-class mechanic without being a good talker, for example. Sometimes the primary job task conflicts with the contact tasks. A surgeon who tried to take phone calls to set up appointments while doing surgery would do a bad job of both, no matter how well the surgeon could do each job separately.

A standard solution to these kinds of problems is to make the contact task a specialized assignment: Hire or designate someone to perform the contact tasks, such as a receptionist at a doctor's office or a "service advisor" at a garage. If the problem is merely a matter of conflicts between doing two things at the same time, a routine can be established so that the contact task is performed only during certain hours of the day.

Drawbacks

The drawbacks to changing contact task assignments are that the changes may mask more serious problems. Just because someone is assigned the task doesn't mean that the task can be done. If the task amounts to coping with conflicting expectations, the person in the job may end up as the chief excuse-giver, or may be in the "hot spot" of absorbing all the heat that results from the conflicting expectations of two units. For example, we might assign one person in the engineering unit the task of responding to calls from the production line, and we might make that person responsible for channeling the problem to the right engineer. Unless the expectations of the supervisor of the engineering unit and his boss, as well as the constraints on the unit, change, however, the person assigned to the new job will just be a nuisance to the other people in the office, causing them to cope with the situation in ways that may cost the company just as much as the old setup did. The job would be a case of dealing with an organizational demand without appropriate power, a situation we will take up in the following section, "Step Two Solutions."

As a rule, don't assign anyone the task of getting someone in another unit to cooperate, agree, coordinate, or to do any kind of "sales job" within the organization. A horrible example of this was found in a large community hospital, which hired a director of medical education and assigned her the job of getting other units to accept education programs for their staff. At no point did the hospital administrator make any effort to support the education programs by making it clear that noncooperation would be frowned upon, or by providing any incentives to the units for accepting education programs, or by making it clear to the unit managers that they would be evaluated negatively for not getting education programs started in their units. Persuasion was the *job* of the medical education director, according to the administrator. The job was, of course, impossible to do. Even the best salesperson, after all, has to be able to offer benefits for the buyer. In this case, all the important benefits were in the hands of the administrator, who wasn't spending them for that purpose!

The step one solutions are ways of changing or clarifying expectations. One question to keep in mind is: What are your expectations and what are the parties' expectations? You can ask whether the new arrangement really clarifies everybody's expectations, whether new conflicts are created (for example, is the person assigned to the contact role properly evaluated and rewarded for it?), or whether the old conflicts are preserved or hidden. The last situation frequently happens when authority is moved up the hierarchy. If the calls from the production line for the engineer are routed through the plant manager's office, the plant manager had better understand which comes first—the reports for the main office or the work to be done on the line—or else the same conflict will occur between the plant manager and the engineering unit over the mixed signals.

In the appendix you will find Worksheet 4—the Step One Solution Sheet—which is a simplified guide to devising pressure point solutions, which you will now be able to use.

Drastic solutions, involving major changes in assignments of supervisors and units, are necessary for many large-scale organizational conflicts. The difficulties with these changes can be very serious, however, so reorganizing is as much a matter of avoiding the creation of new problems as it is of eliminating the sources of conflict that existed in the old setup. An important concern for us in the next few chapters will be how reorganization ideas can go wrong. One thing you learn quickly in dealing with organizational conflicts is that everyone has, or can give, an idea about how things should be rearranged so that people can get their jobs done. What few people can do is to think through the consequences of these suggestions and balance everyone's job again to form a new structure.

To see how to create a new structure it is helpful to have a few rules in mind. The "rules," again, are really lists of reminders about what has to be taken into account in creating a new structure.

The basic formula is this: Organizational conflict usually involves three elements. We will call these three elements

A. Power
B. Organizational demands
C. Worth

Power involves the particular capacities and means that people have at their disposal, in their organizational position, to get their jobs done. To best understand power, think in terms of constraints, of who and what can *keep* a person from getting the job done. Power consists in things like budgetary discretion, personal influence, information, time, space, staff size, dependence on others, and so on. In short, power represents a person's relative autonomy to act freely within the limits set by the organizational context. The key issue is not usually how much power you have, but how it is used. If power is shared, we call this cooperation; if power is withheld or hoarded, we see this as a form of conflict. In an organizational context, too much power can be as bad as too little power when it is used to get the job done without considering all the consequences.

Organizational demands refer to all the expectations that people in an organization have for a person's job performance. By organizational demands we mean those "positive expectations" we have for what others should be doing; if they don't happen or aren't done, we feel disappointed, angry, cheated, or let down by them. These demands are never totally realistic, because we almost always expect more than what will really occur. Making realistic expectations about objective things, such as how many radios a worker can assemble in an hour, is not usually as big a problem as making realistic expectations about less concrete things, such as how much cooperation is expected on a job redesign project. What makes organizational demands difficult to deal with is that people treat us as if we actually can do all things for all people and have them done on time. The real problem emerges when we can't, because other people never blame their faulty expectations; they always blame us for not living up to their dreams—and we do the same with them. Organizational demands have a compelling quality in human relations, so we must treat the question, "What do people expect?" with great respect.

Worth is a general term covering all the things that go into a person's positive self-evaluation. People want the things they do to reflect well on them, and they regard some of the things they do as representing their worth as a human being. Included in these are some things over which the person's superior has control, such as a person's pay, job evaluation, or performance rating, as well as many other things that can be important as proof of worth. Some of these things may seem trivial, such as having an office with a window, or a parking space near the front door; yet if people are denied these things they may feel a loss of "worth." The ultimate power that an organization has to back its demands is the power to deny a person's worth to the organization by firing the person. In this sense, organizational demands and worth are interrelated concepts that we have separated only for the sake of convenience.

There are other sources of worth that are not so directly controlled by management. One that looms large in the managerial tradition of the human relations school of thought is the esteem of one's peers, that is, the way in which co-workers regard the person. Another source of worth, which should never be underestimated, is the intrinsic satisfaction of having a job well done. As we said in Chapter 4, people become possessive about the jobs they do and gain satisfaction from feeling that they do them well. Because these feel-

ings are sometimes completely inscrutable to outsiders, it often becomes a source of organizational problems.

One source of worth that is absent in some situations and completely dominant in others is the professional status of the person. In
many organizations such as universities and hospitals, such things as
rank, pay, and evaluation are controlled by the administration and
don't have much to do with who can tell whom to "buzz-off." Professionals, in short, derive much of their sense of worth from living
up to and succeeding in meeting the standards of their profession or
professional community. If a hospital administrator tells a doctor to
do something that goes against the professional judgment of medi-
cine, the physician will feel a conflict between the two sources of
worth, the organization and the professional community. If the administrator presses the issue, the doctor may act to get rid of the
administrator as a way of resolving the conflict—and may succeed in
doing so.

This illustrates one of the characteristics of conflict. The physician experiences a mismatch between two sources of worth, and he
or she may cope with it by attempting to remove the source of the
mismatch, the administrator. Generally, conflicts result from mis-
matches between power, organizational demands, and sources of
worth. Destructive coping usually results from attempts to produce a
better fit between these elements. The coping mechanisms are
usually the visible feature of the conflict, such as the physician's desire to get rid of the hospital administrator. This coping does not
solve the underlying problem, however, because the hospital will still
need an administrator, and the problem will be recreated again and
again.

Conflicts are resolved by an organizational arrangement that
results in a fit between these three elements. The best way to understand this model of conflict analysis is to apply it to some cases.

Worth-Worth Mismatches

One of the most frequent types of mismatch, or conflict, happens
when a source of esteem for a person, such as her or his immediate
work group, conflicts with another source of feelings of self-worth,
such as a positive relationship with a superior. This particular conflict
causes trouble within the organization when the supervisor tries to

play off the most "loyal" employees against the other employees in the work group, by singling out the "best"—meaning those with whom the supervisor has the best relationship—for special praise and treatment.

One example of this might be called "the case of the teacher's pet," in which the participants were a group of special education teachers who were supposed to work as a team and their supervisor, who was another teacher, had a close relationship with one of the teachers on the team, a relationship that went on beyond work time, as well. The supervisor always gave this teacher the highest evaluations and praise, yet the other teachers in the work group considered her an uncooperative, standoffish, mediocre teacher. Because the supervisor supported this teacher, the group lost trust in the supervisor. The group did not share problems with either the supervisor or the "pet," and these were problems that the supervisor should have been solving. This led to a general loss of the group's effectiveness. The resentment toward the pet increased because she wasn't really pulling her weight in the group, especially in solving the logistical problems. The supervisor, who had lost the trust of the group, therefore lost information on the problems. She coped by thinking that the other teachers were bad and uncooperative, and she was aided in this thought by the coping of the pet, who explained the coldness of the rest of the work group to herself and the supervisor by the conviction that they were inferior and jealous of her. The situation drove the two closer together, and it also drove the rest of the work group together, against the two. This situation is typical of many others in which the peer group and the supervisor are both potential sources of a sense of worth. The relationship with the supervisor should be a source of worth for all of the supervisor's subordinates. If it isn't, if the supervisor fails to give some support of the subordinates' self-worth feelings, the subordinates will be much less happy in their work and will rely more heavily on alternative sources of worth. If these other sources, such as the "esteem of their peers" in the work group, involve a conflicting sense of what the subordinates should be doing to get the job done, this may lead to a more open conflict, and it will definitely lead to a loss of effectiveness in the group. The first rule for belonging to a group is "don't rat"; therefore, the first consequence of the conflict for the supervisor is a loss of information. Fairness on the part of the supervisor doesn't always prevent this conflict from arising, of course. However, a little sensitivity to problems of worth-worth conflicts can be very helpful.

If the problems between a supervisor and a work group are serious, a change in personnel or a rearrangement of the authority relations may be necessary. One method is simply to break up the work group—reassign its tasks and members to other units, and assign the supervisor to a new unit, which then takes on some of the functions of the old units.

Sometimes changing or rearranging personnel is simply not feasible. At upper levels, a halfway solution is to use committee structures. The primary advantage of a committee is that it permits people to say as a group what they could not say as individuals without taking excessive risks. This works only if the committee is functioning as a *committee*, and not as a group in which people make deals for various private advantages. The way to keep this from happening is to make sure that the committees are work groups with defined tasks, and not groups to divide up goodies. If the committee is a task-oriented one, people can take satisfaction in their contributions to it. It becomes a source of worth that substitutes nicely for the problematic source of worth, that is, the supervisor or superior.

In every work setting there are many areas that can be a source of worth for individuals. Different individuals may have different attitudes about what is worthwhile, however, and organizations can polarize situations by forcing people into one camp or another, or they can disregard a person's or group's hard work, thus indicating that their efforts are worthless to the organization. These are the deep-seated problems of worth that can be restructured organizationally.

Power-Power Conflicts

Too much power may seem like a contradiction in terms to the manager who wants as few impediments as possible, but, just as you can't do surgery with a meat-axe because to cut the *right* things you need to feel some resistance, a manager needs to be able to feel resistance, as well. The resistance should be enough that, for example, "good" financial decisions that are also bad production decisions, or "good" production decisions that are also bad financial decisions, won't happen. Ideally, the resistance should come in the form of consultation in which both sides can come to see the issue from the other standpoint.

Frequently power-power conflicts aren't resolved this way. Production and financial units end up fighting a war made possible by the fact that ultimate authority over certain things in production will always rest with production, simply because bookkeepers can't fix machines, and ultimate authority over financial decisions will always rest with the financial officers because they sign the checks.

One way in which this conflict develops is by a power imbalance between the two units, which is then aggravated by upper management decisions that give more power to one unit as a way of "resolving" the conflict. Instead of resolving the conflict, it makes it worse—too little resistance results in too little understanding.

Another way of "resolving" such a conflict, which has the same effect, is to combine in the office of one person power over two tasks which, if each is done properly, should balance the other. This seems like a simple, "tough" solution because the "conflict" stops, and you now hold someone personally responsible, whereas before you could never figure out who was at fault. Sometimes this works, usually when the task performed by one office really hasn't been essential and its resistance has been merely an impediment to the other task. More often it leads to problems in the decision-making process, which then leads to bad decisions.

One example of this is the cocoa manufacturer discussed in Chapter 3. The production officer was the same person as the financial officer, so the production mistake, which ordinarily wouldn't have been covered up, but would simply have been corrected, wasn't corrected for "financial reasons." The combination of powers made it possible for a "good" financial but bad-for-business decision to be covered up by the production officer.

Another example is the university president discussed in Chapter 1 who kept appointing committees until he got the results he wanted. In the long run this kind of excessive use of power leads to a "flunky" attitude on the part of subordinates who then tell the boss only what he or she wants to hear. This often leads directly to conflicts between the boss's supporters and the rest of the people in the organization. One of the limitations of power is that if it is concentrated in the hands of a few people, those people soon find that they become isolated from others. This further limits the effectiveness of their use of power. Even though it makes decision making more complicated by including various points of view, the light-handed use of power is more effective: It makes decision making more realistic, and it creates more support for the decisions that are made.

Organizational Demand–
Organizational Demand Conflicts

Work overloads and conflicting assignments are examples of organizational demand conflicts in which living up to one demand prevents the person from living up to another demand. These in turn produce conflicts when one job has to be sacrificed to get the other one done. In the case of the junior college word processing units in Chapter 3, for example, the employees couldn't both live up to the evaluation expectations of the collegewide word processing center and do the needed work with the audiovisual equipment.

Solving organizational demand–organizational demand conflicts is often difficult, but the basic principle is easy to understand: Don't make conflicting demands in the first place, and change existing conflicting demands so that they no longer conflict. Otherwise, they may lead to conflicts with the people in other units who depend on the performance of the task in order to do their own work.

Unfortunately, many times these conflicts are really beyond the control of the managers. In one food processing company it was necessary to set up a system of holding tanks for waste which would be sold for agricultural purposes. The system required some supervision, but when the main office had agreed to install the system they were told it did not require any additional employees. The plant manager felt he could not lose face by asking for a new employee, so he assigned the job to the supervisor who was in charge of the process located next to the holding tank system. When both the tank system and the process required his attention, he had to sacrifice one or the other. Because the plant process as a whole was continuous, a breakdown in either process might have slowed up the whole plant. The real problem was with the main office. The main office accepted the high-technology production process but did not realize the demands that the technology created. The belief that only a small payroll was required to run the plant was unrealistic, but the plant manager was forced to cope with these expectations. Without sufficient people to monitor the process, there were repeated total shutdowns followed by costly startups. At the plant level, the problem was one of organizational demands, but at the main office level the problem was one of too much power and not enough resistance! This illustrates again how one conflict problem can generate more conflict problems if it isn't dealt with.

Organizational Demand–Worth Conflicts

Organizational demand–worth conflicts ordinarily seem like conflicts between two sources of worth, simply because getting paid and praised for living up to the demands of an organization is an important source of worth.

A work group that is happy and friendly is not necessarily the most efficient or effective work group. Sometimes the personal relations in the work group become such an important source of the sense of worth to the members that the worth that they would derive from meeting the demands of the supervisor or from doing the job well pales into insignificance. Some managers react to this reality by trying to destroy the personal relations within the work group, with the thought that by eliminating these alternative sources of worth the employees become totally dependent on the sources of worth controlled by the organization. The extremes to which managers carry through these efforts at destroying personal relations within the work group to increase production are remarkable.

A particularly grim example is found in the context of win-lose situations. In Chapter 2 we discussed examples of win-lose situations that pitted employees against one another. A cunning variation on this was found in a telephone sales unit of a company that preyed on women in college towns who needed money. The job was to sell tickets to a circus-type event. The sales unit worked in a large room with twenty phones, in four rows of five phones each. The *rows* competed against each other, so that the row with the most sales would be paid a bonus. Later this was varied so that the row with the fewest sales would be fired if it had the fewest sales two days out of the week. You can imagine the effect of this on the employees: If one of them wanted to take a break, she risked losing not only her own job but her row neighbor's as well! And if her neighbor wanted to take a break or to let up on the hard sell, her job was endangered.

The employees worked a few days and then quit. However, the technique worked for the company, which then went on to another area and hired a new set of "salespeople." It could not work for very long. Unless a fresh supply of victims could always be available, the company would run out of employees to do these jobs.

It is easy to imagine the hatred of these employees for their employers. The employees all regarded the supervisor, who sat at a high desk overlooking the phone room, as the very devil himself. If there was a way they could have hurt the supervisor or the company, they would have done so. There wasn't any way to do so in this case, so they quit. However, in most organizations there are plenty of ways for the employees to hurt the organization, so any manager who plays with these techniques is playing with fire.

These jobs are so horrible *because* the job demands destroy the employees' sources of worth. Yet we all have a variety of sources of worth that potentially conflict with the worth that the organization gives us for living up to its demands.

Sources of worth that are intrinsic to the work or to the employee-employer relationship are often overlooked in workplace conflicts, but they can play an important role. In conflicts resulting from work underload, for example, the organization rewards a person without making that person feel "worth it" by doing enough work in return. The phrase "a fair day's work for a fair day's pay" expresses a balancing principle which if violated can cause serious problems. Similarly, an organization that demands that an employee do shoddy work is likely to find that the employees cope with this, not by taking pride in how fast they work, but by feeling contempt for the employer. Much of what gets called "resistance to change" in an organization really is resistance to the loss of this kind of worth, the worth of "a job well done."

Employees faced with a conflict between alternative sources of worth, one that says "do this," and another one that says "don't do it," must choose and then cope with the compromise or choice that is made. The coping behavior may be destructive for the organization, especially when the employees cope by telling themselves that their employer, their co-workers, or the job itself is no good, and that the only reason for staying in the job is to survive for the time being.

The rule in cases of organizational demand–worth conflicts is "don't make assignments of tasks in ways that produce unnecessary worth conflicts." If a big part of an employee's worth is a matter of the status of the position, don't invite trouble by assigning demeaning tasks. If work group relations are a source of value to members, don't expect them to freely give those relations up for the sake of a reorganization plan; expect a fight. An attack on a source of worth, especially if it is a source that is more permanent or less replaceable than a work group, is likely to fail or backfire and turn into destructive coping.

Power Shortage Conflicts

Power–organizational demand conflicts almost invariably have strong "worth" elements as well, and power-worth conflicts almost always involve inappropriate organizational demands, which disrupt ordinary worth-giving human relationships; therefore, we can take up both types together. Because the power problems are usually a matter of not enough power of the right kind, we can call these conflicts "power shortages."

The case of the medical education director we discussed earlier in this chapter is a case of someone making organizational demands without giving the power to meet the demands. The managerial mistake here seems so obvious that one might think that this would not happen very often. But there are some systematic reasons why it happens, and happens often.

When an organization needs a job done and can afford to pay for someone to do it, it seems easy enough to make up a job description that contains the task, hire someone to fill it, and then let the person sink or swim. The problem with this approach is that you don't know that you have a problem until the person starts sinking, but the person won't show it because showing it will cost him or her the job; also, from the higher level manager's point of view, it's hard to tell whether the person is incompetent or whether the job was set up in a way that made it impossible to accomplish. The other reason the mistake of setting up a job without enough power to get it done is so common is that usually the power needed has to come out of someone else's job domain. If you give the medical education director power to set up programs that she sees are needed, you intrude into the authority of the supervisors in whose units the programs are to be given. If the medical education director does not have power, the supervisors won't let her into their units because it implies that their staff is ignorant and "needs educating." If, on the other hand, the education director has lots of power, she can impose her education, but this threatens the supervisor's autonomy. This situation requires a balance between the job demands of the educational director and the sources of power. A balance might be achieved by having the chief hospital administrator tell the supervisors that they *must* have educational programs, but that the supervisors themselves will be permitted to determine the topics and scheduling of the sessions and to work with the educational director to provide the teaching. In this way power and demands might be balanced by creating the demand for educational programs and also by allowing them to fit into the existing system of organization.

So many, in fact most, *new* positions are underpowered, and many of these remain that way. If the jobs also serve as entry positions, the problem may not be too noticeable, because people will move out of the job rather than complain. Also, if no one is quite sure how the task should be performed because there are no traditional standards or past performances with which to compare, the position may never be a source of overt conflict; however, the job won't be done, either, and moving on as a way of coping with this may have destructive side effects.

The rule here is this: Don't assign a task without giving or creating the necessary means. In practice, this means that new tasks should be reviewed carefully as they develop to see whether the necessary powers are there. It may be convenient to blame the occupant of the position when the job isn't getting done, but in the long run it's better to make sure the powers given to a position match the task.

In practice matching powers to the task may turn out to be very difficult. Some powers exist only to force others in the organization to take the requirements of a task seriously. The form this may take is no more complicated than granting the person in the position the right to complain about noncooperation to the next level manager. The play back and forth may become very complicated. The aim in giving powers to a position is not to abolish this play, but to provide the conditions for the development of a good working relationship where everyone can perform the needed tasks.

The general rule relating to power and organizational demands is this: Don't give power without responsibility, and don't give responsibility without power. If someone is given a power, there must be some organizational check on the use of that power. If someone has the power to impede someone else in the performance of his or her job, there should be a means—an evaluation or feedback device—that can regulate the use of that power. When the engineering unit decides to send in a report on time rather than deal with a process problem, those workers should be evaluated accordingly, by some evaluation input from the process units themselves, or by a method of assessing costs of engineering-related process problems.

CONCLUSION

The last rule to remember in redoing a setup is "if it doesn't itch, don't scratch." Don't disrupt any working relationship to fit into some abstract model of how an organization should work, even if the abstract model in question is the organization chart of your own organization, which, one must always remember, does not describe many of the working relationships that do exist in the organization. Formal rules, task assignments, new evaluation procedures, and so on are like the pins that are put in broken bones. They allow bones to grow. If they don't grow properly, then it is time to break them and try again. Management is like surgery. It is the task of using power for promoting healthy working relationships, which the organization needs to grow and become strong enough to survive the natural shocks of personnel change, change in the environment of the organization, and changes in leadership directions.

Power, organizational demands, and worth are not elements acting alone, but elements that can help describe the underlying qualities of the working relationships that make up an organization. When the work routine of an organization is changed, so is the relationship between these underlying elements. It is possible, therefore, to make organizational relations better. We do not have to accept the worst if we are aware of the real issues underlying the relationships that create conflict.

In the appendix you will find five work sheets with questions that will be useful in helping you to understand particular types of conflict, and to consider solutions. These questions are not a litmus test. They are designed to be used in the light of your judgment and best knowledge of the people in the situation. The questions are called "Guide Questions" because they are meant to guide your thinking—not to be a substitute for thinking!

SOME PITFALLS
OF REORGANIZATION:
FORESEEING
THE FORESEEABLE

THE UNWELCOME TONIC

Reorganization plans are not always popular when they are presented as solutions to problems of conflict. When a reorganization plan is announced, administrators are often stunned by the fact that employees may not only not welcome the new ideas, but may respond with great suspicion and anxiety. Yet reorganization is a natural part of organizational life. Organizations are operating in a changing world with all kinds of new situations arising that the organization has to adjust to if it is going to prosper.

In an already functioning organization, successful reorganization involves dealing with four elements: First, there must be a *recognition* of a problem that is related to the operating mode of the organization; second, there should be a *plan* that is designed to relieve or eliminate the problems of the organization; third, and often overlooked, the *attitudes* of those people who must implement the reorganization plan must change. (The change, to succeed, must have something positive in it for everyone. When the implementers are not the planners, there is a heightened potential for misunderstanding and disagreement about what the reorganization process should entail); fourth, and finally, there must be *new outcomes* in the organization process—the old problems must be eliminated and, ideally, new problems will be anticipated.

Because reorganization is so important for the effective operation of any company, one might suspect that there is a great deal known about the pitfalls of reorganization. When we look into the matter however, we realize that very little has been written about the conflicts and shortcomings caused by various strategies of reorganization. The reason for this is probably a natural outcome of the reorganization process itself. When plans for reorganization are announced, exaggerated promises are generally made that these new reforms will solve all the old problems, will increase efficiency, and will cut costs dramatically. One of the characteristics of reorganization is that the intended effects are almost always oversold. Therefore, any serious drawbacks in the plan or major failures tend to be papered over and the plan is usually talked about as if it were a brilliant success. When was the last time you heard a company president admit that the company's reorganization plan was a complete disaster that created far more problems than it was supposed to solve? When reorganization plans fail, people simply call for another reorganization, and they seldom take time to analyze the failures.

There are several reasons why reorganization plans are not always welcomed by the employees who have worked hard to make the old organizational system function. The employees may feel that their efforts were in vain now that the top brass wants to reorganize. Employees may say, "I have worked hard on this job for years, and reorganization is all the thanks I get." Many people have fears of what change will bring. Often, departments begin to scramble and compete for power and influence as soon as a reorganization plan is announced. The idea that certain jobs may be eliminated or that certain jobs may lose their importance and status in an organization represents a tremendous threat to people who have invested their careers in a particular job or job track. It is important to note that these hurt feelings and insecurities may not be easily smoothed over. Remember that the old form of organization represented work habits that were built up over time, and that these work habits are the familiar and reliable way that people have learned to do their jobs, and are important sources of worth. To remove these familiar and reliable patterns of work and meaningful sources of worth to substitute a new form of organization understandably causes people a great deal of insecurity. The reorganization process itself, then, must include ways of dealing with people's feelings of insecurity.

Reorganization plans also tend to cause various people and various departments within a company to begin taking sides. Some departments may feel that the reorganization plan will help them, will give them more importance in the company's operations, will make their jobs easier, or will increase their function. These departments are quick to line up in favor of reorganization. On the other side, however, other departments may feel that the reorganization slights them or does not give them an important enough role in company affairs. Although these departments will not openly resist the reorganization plan, they may withhold their cooperation and make sure that they are not assigned blame for any of the shortcomings of the reorganization plan. It is safe to say that if a large number of employees do not accept a reorganization plan, the plan is doomed to failure. Yet many managers believe that it is not really necessary to sell the idea of reorganization to their own employees. Sometimes these managers will, under the banner of improving communication, go through the ritual of asking advice or having groups fill out questionnaires, but not really deal with the problems of fear and insecurity or the taking of sides that occur at the first stage of any reorganization. Because of this indifference to the employees' fears, the process of reorganization can be a boneyard of good ideas that were never properly implemented.

Let us for a moment set aside the problem of the simple resistance to change that may occur with the announcement of a reorganization plan and focus on some of the pitfalls that appear when certain reorganization strategies are attempted. The pitfalls discussed in this chapter and the next chapter are presented as examples of some of the potential problems that can arise in any reorganization plan. These pitfalls *are* foreseeable, and they can be avoided, but it takes effort and thought.

The Example of Delegated Authority

One of the popular forms of reorganization has been to delegate authority and responsibility to subordinates within an organization in an attempt to decentralize its operations. The idea of delegating authority, on the face of it, seems like a reform that will increase the efficiency and effectiveness of the organization, because many of the small daily problems can be solved without increasing paperwork or creating needless delays waiting for approval. Another purpose of delegating authority is to permit wider participation in the decision-making process. Thus, the motivation behind these changes is usually a good one. The existing structure creates conflicts by concentrating too many powers in the same position or office. The conflicts—which are chronic in "American-style" organizations—are what we called power-power conflicts in the last chapter.

The basic idea of a power-power conflict bears repeating, both because it is difficult and because it is so important. As in many other organizational phenomena, it can be understood by comparing it to occurrences in families. If you have children, you know what happens when, as a parent, you intrude too much into their disputes, as an adjudicator or a side-taker. What usually happens is that you start getting bad information. The child who thinks you will side with her turns into a tattletale, and the tales begin to get exaggerated and possibly false. The other child may just shut off the relationship with you, for his own protection, leaving it at a formal level so that he won't get unfairly punished, or he may respond by getting angry and taking it out on you, or on the other child, or maybe on the family dog. The child may also go to the other parent for support.

All of these bad consequences have their analogues in organizations. They all flow from the overuse of authority. The worst consequence, especially from the point of view of productivity, is for trust and cooperation between subordinates to disappear. When children are let alone, they tend to work things out: when a parent steps in, to decide how they should play together or to make other decisions for them, cooperation very often goes out the window. Why should this be? The reasons are fairly simple. Cooperation and trust cannot be dictated. They must grow, and growing means *allowing* them to grow, and, sometimes, creating conditions that allow them to grow.

With children, it is easy to see what it means to create conditions that allow trust and cooperation to grow. It means allowing the children to realize and deal—in their own way—with the fact that the happiness of each depends on the happiness of the other. When the parent steps in and makes decisions relating to the child's happiness, decisions about what is "fair" or what the child should be doing, the "fact" of mutual dependence is no longer a "fact"; instead, the parent creates a new fact of dependence on the parent.

Unfortunately, this kind of dependent relationship can be ego-gratifying for the parent, who is always "needed" by the child. The "need," of course, is a created need, created by the parent who makes the child dependent. The same thing happens with the manager who makes the success of the subordinate or the unit dependent on doing favors or taking the side of the subordinate or unit. The manager is "needed" all the time because he or she has created a situation in which it is easier for the subordinate to succeed by calling on the higher level manager than by developing a relation of trust and cooperation with others on whom the successful doing of the job depends.

When the relations between subordinates involve working out rules or procedures, the enforcement of rules and procedures, or goal setting, the intrusive manager creates a serious problem. Some goals, and some rules, are likely to favor one unit or subordinate against another. When several units or subordinates must work the rules or goals out together, each is in a position to make the best judgments about what is important to get and what can be given in return to the others. Between subordinates, the issue is a matter of coming to mutually advantageous solutions. The intrusive manager, in a power-power position, changes the issue by virtue of the fact that this manager does not delegate power. The issue changes to "what kind of deal can you get out of the manager?" Of course, in the game of getting a good deal from the big boss, the best boot-licker or showperson often wins. The quality of information shared with the top will also go down, just as, when you intrude into the lives of your children and announce that you will decide something, the quality of information you get from your children will also go down—right down to wheedling, lies, distortions, tattling, and so on. Although it may be true that, in general, you are older, wiser, and a better decision-maker than your children, you can't make good decisions with bad information. Thus, by intruding you create conditions that prevent you from using your wisdom!

Too much power, too many powers, and power applied too frequently is self-defeating. So many organizations, recognizing this, decentralize and delegate. Of course, in many cases the delegation of authority is in name only. The central authority maintains control, and participation by subordinates is more of a ritual than a reality. The delegation of authority that takes the form of "the boss won't tell you what to do, but you will be responsible for reading his mind" makes participants feel that the delegation of authority is a sham. However, even if a considerable amount of authority is genuinely transferred, a number of problems may arise.

Coordination Problems

If several departments within a company are delegated greater authority to run their own operations, this may reduce the coordination of activities between departments. Different departments are naturally interested in and responsible for different things, and they may be reluctant to spend time and resources helping out another department on tasks that they feel are not really a central part of their own operation. When authority is centralized this problem can be solved simply by the boss's telling them to cooperate, or else. When authority is delegated, then cooperation must come from the negotiated tradeoffs that department heads work out. If one department head feels that it is the responsibility of the other department head to cooperate with him or her without giving anything in return for this cooperation, then organizational conflict can arise because decentralization has changed the rules of organizational cooperation.

Facing Responsibility

A second problem that occurs with decentralization comes from the fact that subordinates can no longer hide behind the responsibility of the boss or the central office. Centralization always facilitates the transfer of blame from a department to the central administrators of the company. Generally there exists a sort of "we–they" relationship, so that people in a department can say, "We would like to help you, but 'they' are stopping us." Subordinates may have gotten used to hiding behind the boss by saying, "I'd like to help, but the boss would kill me," whenever tough decisions came up or unpleasant demands were made on them. With decentralization they must face these problems and solve the problems themselves. When a reorganization plan is set forth that calls for the delegation of authority, the employees may feel very happy about being able to control their own work situation, but they may learn later on that it is not very pleasant to face the pressures and get blamed for the consequences of their performance.

Settling Disagreements

A third problem that comes from the delegation of authority is one of settling disagreements. Individuals in an office have differing opinions about what to do and how to do it. With the delegation of authority this may create conflict because these disagreements are brought out by the greater participation in decision making. Under the old system of centralized authority these disagreements did not surface because the system of authority worked on the principle that whatever the boss says goes. With decentralization you have removed this central authority, and now you must create a way to establish agreement on management policies without creating too many hurt feelings. Management may need to set up consensus-building procedures *before* it delegates authority, so that decisions will be made in an appropriate consensual way by workers where previously no consensus was called for by the work situation. Nevertheless, the delegation of authority almost always causes workers to discover the painful fact that many conflicts have been lying under the surface in their own units.

Career Fear

A fourth problem with the delegation of responsibility is the creation of "career fear." With the delegation of responsibility, suddenly employees are faced with changes in the standards of their job evaluations. When they had a "boss," the problems were relatively simple; now they may not be sure as to exactly what is expected of them. The new freedom implied in the delegation of responsibility can create a tremendous amount of new anxiety in employees who are afraid that they are going to be blamed for many things for which they were previously not responsible. In addition, career fear may be heightened by the fact that with the delegation of responsibility the old steps in the promotion system are changed. It may no longer be clear to employees what job changes constitute promotion and what job changes constitute lateral moves. The process of delegating authority may change the employees' perception of what positions are good positions to be in for future promotion. Some of these career fear problems can be sidestepped by just giving employees a pay raise as part of the reorganization because of the increased responsibility that they are getting. This is a way of buying time so that some of these fears will subside.

The fact that some of these pitfalls in the process of delegating authority create problems that can often be solved by consolidating authority accounts for the fact that many organizations over a period of years go through reorganization plans that delegate authority, followed by other reorganization plans that centralize authority. When real delegation takes place, however, some of these problems can be solved by creating specific mechanisms for coordinating activities, correcting mistakes, resolving conflicts, and specifying methods of evaluation and promotion patterns.

Feedback That Backfires

One of the themes of the last section was that organizational conflicts *and* the reorganization process invariably involve problems of bad information. In this section we will take up the general problem of the information process in an organization. The issues here are part of the daily life of any organization, whether it is reorganizing, or facing conflicts, or doing neither. The problem of information is always heightened in conflict and reorganization situations, however, and many times the standard methods for getting the necessary information simply don't work.

One standard method for getting necessary information, used especially by organizations committed to Organizational Development, is the creation of a feedback system, usually involving questionnaires and various kinds of performance measures. Organizational feedback gets its name from automatic control systems used to regulate the operations of machines in which two operations are interdependently linked in a relationship of mutual cause and effect. In a strictly mechanical system the operation of one machine regulates the operation of the other machine and vice versa. This is what engineers call a "closed loop." Feedback systems are described as systems in which the output of an activity is dependent on another system's input. The concept of feedback is useful for understanding the interdependence of organizational operations, because often the operations of organizations appear to be similar to mechanical feedback loops. Both mechanical and organizational feedback systems have similar shortcomings, and these are important to understand in interpreting the "feedback" information.

Inflexibility of the Closed Loop

One of the limitations of feedback systems is that they must be designed around standardized responses. If machine A increases its output, machine B must be signaled to do the same. If machine B fails to increase its speed, then machine A must be signaled to shut down. In either case the actions and the responses must all be programmed ahead of time. This is also true in human organizations. The behavior of all of the actors involved in the feedback system must be reduced to a limited set of actions and responses. A feedback system is ideal for coordinating routine work operations, but it breaks down entirely if any parts of the system are confronted with a *new problem*. For example, one might construct a system of radar that would coordinate the landings and takeoffs of a large municipal airport. Each airplane would be told on the basis of the amount of traffic exactly at what speed, at what altitude, and from what direction to approach the airport. As planes approached the airport, they would be assigned a place in the landing order, and as planes were loaded at the airport they would be assigned a place in the takeoff order; all of these events could thus be routinely handled. Yet what would happen in such a case if there were an accident on one of the runways, but the system continued to instruct airplanes to continue landing on that runway in the order in which they were originally programmed to arrive? Without some way of breaking the closed loop of a feedback system, the system would continually feed the disaster with more and more airplanes landing on top of each other. Although contingency plans can be programmed into the system, the number of such contingencies must be limited. Thus, feedback systems cannot completely replace more flexible forms of organization that can take into consideration "unprogrammable" major changes in circumstances.

Imbalance in the Loop

A second problem with feedback systems is that all feedback systems contain within them some degree of error. Usually this is in the form of a time lag between the response of one of the parts of the system and the reaction by other parts of the system. An example would be the relationship in a manufacturing company between the sales and production departments. If there were a considerable time lag between the sales reports and the production scheduling, you could find yourself in a situation where you do not have the goods to sell because production has fallen behind sales, or you could find yourself in a situation where the level of sales has dropped off and production has continued, thereby causing overproduction. Getting a correct balance between sales and production implies that the time lag between sales information and production scheduling should not be too great. On the other hand, if the coordination between sales and production is too tight, so that until a salesman sells an order nothing is produced, this situation may force clients to wait too long for their product. Adjusting a feedback system so that there is a tolerable level of error between the actions of one unit and the reactions of the other is important to achieve if conflict in the organization is to be kept at a minimum.

The problem of feedback error can also be heightened by an uneven response. Many times in a feedback loop one side will begin to overreact or underreact to the stimulus of the other party in the loop. As a consequence, you could be faced with a situation in which you may get too much feedback too soon, or too little too late. A typical example of this might be found in an organization where a top administrator sends a request down the hierarchy for some small job to be done, and the subordinates drop everything that they are doing to satisfy the request. The administrator may find out weeks later that nothing else has gotten done, and when they are asked why not, the subordinates may simply reply, "You told us to do this other project." This kind of exaggerated response in human organizations is one of the problems inherent in any feedback relationship in which there is a marked difference in power and authority between the two actors.

Overreaction to Feedback

A third limitation of feedback systems is that of self-excitation. The actors in a feedback loop can begin acting and reacting to each other in such a way that both sides overproduce at a frenzied rate. Like a puppy chasing its tail, the system is self-stimulating. The cycles of a feedback system can become vicious circles. Suppose a company devises a scheme of information feedback about the activities of the employees throughout the work day. From this data, managers find out that many of the employees are not following the operating policies of the company. This bit of information leads the managers to decide to add additional policies to plug the gaps and loopholes in the old operating policies. However, the new policies that have now been made more complex are more difficult for employees to follow, so that *more* employees are found to be not following the policies in doing their jobs. The administrators react by adding more policies. The vicious circle continues until the employees find themselves in the position where if they are going to do their jobs, they cannot follow policy, and if they follow policy, they will never get their jobs done. In the case of this kind of vicious circle the reaction to feedback information causes the administrators to exaggerate the problem rather than stabilize the problem.

Manipulation of Feedback

One of the uses of the concept of feedback is to describe systems that attempt to provide information to individuals so that they will adapt and modify their behavior in the organization. If the desired aim of performance feedback is to modify the individual's behavior and to motivate the individual to work more effectively, then performance feedback often produces some undesirable side effects. One of the most common side effects of performance feedback is that individuals begin to act in terms of the interests created by the performance standard set for their individual job, rather than act in the interests of the company. This individualization can produce a harmful competition among employees to see who can get the best performance statistics. In addition, individuals often sabotage the feedback process by becoming self-serving manipulators of feedback information. Because the feedback process is totally dependent on *effective communications*, that is, the transfer of information from one person to another with as little distortion as possible, the manipulation of information to create certain impressions can render the feedback process useless.

An example of manipulation of the feedback mechanism would be with the performance feedback mechanism used in company sales in which each salesperson and the group of salespeople are given a report each month on the volume of sales and whether they are above or below the yearly sales targets that have been set. This information feedback is designed to let the salespeople know if they are falling below sales targets; hopefully, if they are below their sales targets they will redouble their efforts. Several years ago in a conversation with a salesperson in the last financial quarter of the year, the salesperson was asked, "How's business?" The reply was that business was terrible. The other people in the conversation said that that was too bad. The salesperson said no, that was good, because it looked as if the volume of sales for the year would be down 18 or 20 percent from the sales target. The others asked the salesperson why that was good. The reply was that when you are having a difficult year, if you work hard and miss the sales target by one percent, management says, "What's the matter with you guys, you're not working hard enough?" But if you are having a difficult year and you miss the target by 15 or 20 percent, everybody assumes that there is something wrong with the market and that the sales force was doing the best it could. This means that they will lower the sales target for the next year, and at the same time the salespeople will all predate their orders in the last financial quarter so that it will look as if the sales were made during the next fiscal year. This way, next year they will easily make the sales target.

This example points up one of the problems of performance feedback that must be kept in mind: Feedback information is always subject to interpretation. In the case of the sales example, once the salespeople saw it would be difficult to make their sales target, they decided to make sure that they missed the target by a wide mark, and at the same time, they stockpiled some of their sales orders so that the first quarter of the new financial year would be a resounding success. The important thing to remember is that people do not simply receive information like machines; they interpret it. Any set of simple facts can have dozens of different interpretations.

Meaningless Feedback

The use of feedback as an information process to solve organizational problems has often taken the form of distributing some sort of questionnaire or attitude inventory. The questionnaire method of information gathering is often used by top administrators as a mechanism for "employee input" into decision making as well as a diagnostic tool for discovering and solving problems. In most cases the use of questionnaires does none of these things. In the first place, managers often find the use of questionnaires a threat, because it implies that the employees have all the answers and that managers do not know what is going on in their section of the company. Therefore administrators are often eager to throw the results of questionnaire studies in the wastebasket and go back to their own methods of administration. In the second place, employees are self-conscious about the information output that they give to their superiors. The work situation may create for its employees the need to "look good," and therefore employees may fill out questionnaires in such a way that their answers do not accurately reflect the feelings and problems encountered in their daily work. Furthermore, because most people have had experience in filling out questionnaires that have no relevance to their daily lives, employees may find the process of filling out questionnaires demeaning and therefore not worthy of careful and honest thought. Often the designers of questionnaires are apt to ask employees whether they are happy or unhappy, as if the answers to that question were sufficient so that the designer of the questionnaire may avoid asking *what* is making people unhappy in the job situation. Employees who are asked such general questions as "Are you happy?" may feel that management is not taking their feelings very seriously unless they are asked some specific questions about which aspects of their work make them unhappy. Many questionnaires are not designed to feed back information about how the organization operates. They are often designed to feed back the beliefs and feelings of employees, and employees are quick to note that their beliefs and feelings are not going to improve their work situation. The employees may thus simply tell management that they are happy with their jobs. Many workers feel that if management actually wants to know how things are operating and what the workers' problems are, they will respect them enough to come and ask, and that filling out a questionnaire is a meaningless gesture. The point here is that information output from employees in the form of questionnaire responses is subject to a variety of interpretive biases, depending on the basic organizational relationships, so that these relationships create their own smokescreens; thus, information feedback systems may contain very little real information.

CONCLUSION

How do you get meaningful information? Unfortunately, there is no one-step answer to this question. Indeed, the problem is a "Catch-22." To produce a situation in which you can get good information, you must create an organization in which there is trust, mutual respect, and cooperation. To create this organization, you need to do things that eliminate conflict, mutual suspicion, and destructive competition between units and managers. To do this successfully, however, requires good information.

Again, the situation is much like a family. There is no one thing you can do or announce that will produce an honest sharing of feelings and information between you and your children or between you and your spouse. Whatever you do or announce will be interpreted in terms of the old, conflict-ridden way. You *can* gradually develop a situation of trust and cooperation. As the conflicts diminish, the information improves. You have to start somewhere, however, and the best place to start is with your own actions and words.

7

THE CREATION
OF NEW CONFLICTS

Reorganization, which rearranges rules and jobs, may eliminate conflicts only at the cost of creating new conflicts. Indeed, there are some places in the reorganization process where this happens frequently. In this chapter we will discuss the two primary places where reorganization creates new conflict. The first is the area of the application of new rules. The second is the area of job design.

NEW RULES

Some of the types of new conflict created by changes are familiar: They are the worth, power, and organizational demand conflicts discussed in Chapter 5. Another type of problem results from the fact that the old rules had an oral tradition that surrounded the rules, which provided stories and precedents to guide the application of a particular rule in unusual situations and provided some guidance in deciding how important the fine details of the rule were. With a new rule, of course, there is no specific tradition relating to the particular rule; employees are often left to apply the rule either mechanically or too strictly, or to use the rule in light of their own general experience with company rules and the old aims and purposes of the company.

Rules and Routine

The creation of new rules, policies, and procedures for doing all of the different jobs within the organization is one of the important aspects of any plan for reorganization. Every organization needs its operating rules so that it will operate in a reasonably predictable and uniform way. The uniformity that rules create is a uniformity in the outcomes of different people's work and a uniformity in the behavior of employees. The rules of an organization create both the means and the ends for doing all the various jobs. Reorganization often requires the creation of new sets of rules in the form of policies and procedures that will be used to change the pattern of work in the organization. Changing people's behavior, however, even their rule-following behavior, is not always easy. Reorganization requires a breaking of the old routine, with the promise of creating a new routine for doing the work. By breaking a routine, you are asking people to give up familiar habits and, even more important, the certainty that comes from knowing exactly what the outcome will be if certain routine procedures are followed. Reorganization always creates a degree of uncertainty about exactly what the outcomes will be if the new rules are followed. The rules that make a work routine are the rules that are taken for granted and accepted without question, and this is where their power to influence people's behavior lies. When employees examine a new set of rules, policies, and procedures for doing their jobs, they immediately question the adequacy of these strange procedures and begin to speculate about, "What if this happens? What if that happens?" Untried rules do not promise predictable outcomes, and employees are apt to use the new rules from a reorganization plan in the most self-protective fashion, thereby creating burdensome red tape. Reorganization requires learning new work habits, and as with any other set of habits, it may require forgetting the old procedures for doing the work. Learning a new work routine may be as difficult as learning to write with your toes; it can be done, but it takes time and persistence.

When reorganizing, you must plan in terms of how many procedures you would be asking employees to forget as well as how many new procedures you would be requiring them to learn. The most radical reorganization would be a total substitution calling for completely forgetting how the work used to be done and learning an entirely new work routine. A reorganization that is a total substitution of the new for the old will require more time, persistence, and daily problem solving than will a reorganization that calls for only a partial substitution of new rules and procedures for old ones. One of the problems with a partial substitution of rules is that the change often occurs slowly, over a period of time, which involves the buildup of a certain amount of inconsistency between the new rules and procedures and the old, familiar routine. These inconsistencies are usually resolved by the employees in an informal way, thus creating a situation in which supervisors may not know how things are actually being done, and in which the only way new employees can learn the job is by experience and with the help of older employees. Reorganization can thus actually increase the employee reliance on experience rather than on written policies.

The Elements of a Rule

Putting aside, for the moment, the problem of total or partial reorganization, let's focus on the problem of rules. It's misleading to think that a rule always gives you a specific routine and a certainty about the outcome of the work. Many things can go wrong when you start changing rules to reorganize a department of a company, and some of these problems stem from the way human beings are accustomed to using the rules. It is important to remember the old saying, "Some people follow some of the rules some of the time, but no one follows all of the rules all of the time." This saying suggests that people are selective about which rules they think should be followed and who should be required to follow them. What do we mean by a "rule," anyway? An organizational rule might be defined as *a general instruction to a group or category of employees to perform (or not perform) certain activities on certain occasions.* An organizational rule has three important elements: 1) the performance of an activity, 2) the appropriate occasion for performing it, and 3) some specification as to which people the rule applies to. Each of these three elements can cause problems for reorganization.

The first element of a rule, which refers to performance of an activity, is probably the simplest one to deal with. Usually new rules and procedures can be learned by a simple training program in which the rules and procedures are explained and people are expected to rehearse the correct procedures as they are called for in the new policy. This means, of course, that the training will take time and will disturb the routine of the work setting, but it is usually worthwhile in terms of creating consistency in the reorganization efforts. The training program also provides an opportunity to iron out potential conflicts that might arise in the implementation of any new set of rules or policies.

The other two elements present problems in reorganization that aren't so easy to solve, in the short run, at least. The second element, which refers to applying the rule and procedure at the appropriate occasion, brings up a problem that can only be partially solved by retraining the employees. A procedure that is applied at the wrong time under the wrong circumstances is a worthless activity. By specifying a particular activity, a rule or policy in effect eliminates all other possible activities that might be done within a given situation. This can be illustrated by using a simple example. Assume that an organizational rule says that "all purchase orders must be approved and signed by Mr. Jones." This rule represents a simple organizational rule that centers purchasing authority in one man, that is, Mr. Jones. When your department wants to purchase something, this rule applies, and it is understood that Mr. Jones's authority refers only to purchasing power. If employees follow the rule too literally, however, then when Mr. Jones goes for his three weeks' vacation in the summer, the company will be unable to purchase any materials. If there is no rule that covers this contingency, then how do department heads purchase necessary items? They must rely on experience, which tells them which individuals in the organization can approve purchases when Mr. Jones is absent. The point here is that how a rule is to be applied in a given situation cannot always be specified, and that a person must learn from experience how a rule is to be used in a wide variety of situations. The problem for reorganization is that experience does not come with the writing of new rules, so a department may be thrown into chaos the minute there is the slightest block in procedures. This is like telling a new boiler room employee to shut off the fire under the boilers when the pressure gets too high, when only experience can tell an employee how high the pressure can get in the boilers. The consequence of the rule in this case will probably be that your worker will sit around waiting for the explosion. No set of rules can specify all of the possible contingencies that limit when a rule should be applied and when it should be ignored. Unfortunately, new rules do not come with ready-made experience built into them.

The third element of rules and procedures deals with those employees to whom the rule applies. A policy usually specifies fairly clearly which employees are expected to engage in what activities; it therefore specifies the group of employees to whom the rule applies. The rule that "all purchase orders must be approved and signed by Mr. Jones" applies to all the individuals in the company who are allowed to make out purchase orders. One presumes that not every worker in the company will have this task as part of his or her responsibility. Thus the rule defines a set of employees who are obliged to follow it. This can cause two problems for reorganization. First, a rule is always an external check on an employee's actions. The following of a rule is a way of watching, monitoring, or checking on an employee's behavior. New rules that require employees' actions to be monitored or checked may therefore create a certain amount of resentment; for example, department heads may feel that Mr. Jones has no business telling them what they need to buy and what they don't need to buy. The formation of new rules may thus be seen by department heads as an activity that undermines their authority and autonomy to do their job or as an implication that they are not doing their job in a "cost conscious" manner. The second aspect that can cause problems in reorganization deals with the fact that rules change the way in which people work together. It is generally true that people with high status and authority within an organization are in a position to tell people of lower status and authority what to do, and that people of lower status and authority in a company tend to follow procedures or wait to be told what to do. Therefore, to go back to our example of the rule that applies to purchasing authority, Mr. Jones may feel that he is the servant of his subordinates because they are constantly coming in and demanding his approval for the purchase of items that are needed in a rush. In the more extreme example, rules that apply to parking privileges, dress codes, or the use of expense accounts may define a particular status for a group of employees; any change in these rules caused by reorganization may cause bad feelings on the part of those employees who are excluded from the group that was originally defined by the rule.

Rule Following and the Oral Tradition

So a rule specifies the performance of a particular activity on an appropriate occasion by certain employees. Now we need to make one more distinction about rules and people's behavior in organizations. We tend to think that people should follow rules, without considering very carefully what we really want people to do. If people simply follow rules without thinking or using their own discretion, then we often find people doing "the right thing in the wrong situation." This can cause considerable conflict in an organization. Blind, mindless rule following is a central problem to bureaucratic administration, and it is also one of the things we hate most about the use of rules in an organization. Employees soon learn that they can hide behind the rules for self-protection, but this does not always produce effective results. Reorganization can cause employees to feel uncertain and ill at ease, so they follow the rules explicitly in a self-protective way, but in doing so, they may cause the whole department or organization to grind to a halt. If we don't want employees to simply follow rules, then the question is, What do we really want them to do? We really want the employees to "act in consideration of the rules" so that their actions are effective in coordinating the activities and work of the organization. To act in consideration of a rule is to take into account the specific conditions and the probable outcome of one's actions, rather than blindly follow the procedures that the rule prescribes. For employees to act in consideration of rules rather than to just follow rules requires that they feel some degree of security in the outcome of their actions and that their actions will be understood by others as "doing the best they can."

Stated another way, employees must interpret rules. In doing this, they often rely on what we might call the "oral tradition" of the organization—the folklore, precedents, and past experiences involving questions of how to apply, when to apply, and when to ignore the rules. Often a large part of "learning the job" is a matter of learning this oral tradition. With new rules this highly necessary oral tradition is strained—it doesn't vanish, but it has to be expanded and stretched to fit the new rules. Usually this straining amounts to reinterpreting the new rules in light of what the oral tradition says about the aims of the organizations, the intentions of superiors, and the needs of employees who must follow the rules for protection from the various bad consequences that can come from interpreting the rules in the wrong way, that is, too strictly or too lightly. Of course, the establishing of an oral tradition takes time—long enough for stories to generate about what happens if you interpret the rules in the wrong way.

The oral tradition may sometimes subvert any new changes. An interesting example of this was an attempt in a very large international corporation to upgrade a particular unit. The unit had administrative functions within the company and consequently could not be evaluated on the usual profit-and-loss basis. The managerial tradition of the company was that promotions went to "stars," that is, managers who had good profit figures in their units, so this unit was obviously not a place to become a star. It had usually been headed by an executive whose career had peaked, who was not expected to move up, and whose best and safest strategy was simply not to make big mistakes. This strategy translated into "don't make any major expenditures." So the unit worked with antiquated technology and outdated practices, but it did its job, in the minimal way that was expected of it in the company, and no one got into trouble.

The company soon got a new chief executive officer (C.E.O.) who had just come from a firm in which the operations of this same type of unit had been aggressive, successful, and industry-leading; he was a generally acknowledged contributor to the success of that company. When the C.E.O. took over, he decided to upgrade the unit; so he put one of the rising stars in charge of the unit, giving him carte blanche. In particular, the new head of the unit was expected to make major expenditures for new technology, which was essential to upgrading procedures and results.

The new head of the unit spent his first ten months on the job in a dither of pricing new tools, learning about other, more advanced companies' methods, and traveling all over the world to get information on company needs that might be filled by an upgraded unit of this type.

On returning from one of these trips, the new head of the unit called the company purchasing department to check on how his purchase orders were progressing and when the new equipment would begin arriving. To his shock, he was told that the purchasing department had no purchase orders. He called in his equipment manager, whose task it had been to fill out the purchase orders and attend to details.

The equipment manager, a veteran of many years with the company, was steeped in its oral tradition. He saw it as his job to protect the head of his unit from stupid mistakes. The previous unit heads had usually been appreciative of this—they understood that the only thing that mattered to them, at that point in their careers, was not to make mistakes that might cost them their jobs.

The equipment manager calmly told the new head that he hadn't placed the orders. He went on to say that this sort of thing had never been done before, and that he was just protecting the both of them against the trouble that would surely come when someone in an upper-level position looked at their expenditures. "They'll just say, 'you're young, you don't know any better and you're fired.' But they'll say to me, 'you're supposed to know something—where the hell did you get the idea that you could spend ten times what you spent last year?' They won't fire me—they'll send me to the funny-farm." He then pointed out that the unit never was a high priority for the company, and that he'd never been told that things had changed.

The head of the unit was furious, but he knew that the equipment manager was a well-intentioned person, so he went straight to the C.E.O. to explain the problem. The problem was solved only by an elaborate public performance for the unit by the C.E.O., who pledged his support for the head of the unit, provided assurances about his intentions to make the unit an industry leader, and so on.

The difficulty here stems from the fact that formal organizational demands always have to be interpreted. The interpretation is made on the basis of an oral tradition, which tells what the meaning of the rules and demands "really is," or what it is "in practice." Usually these interpretations help the organization along by filling in the gaps in the rules, making consistent that which isn't quite consistent, assuring continuity, and protecting people when breaking the rules is necessary. Without these interpretations, organizational life would be impossible because no one can write enough rules to cover enough circumstances so that *no* interpretation is necessary. But the interpretations—the oral tradition—may conflict with the aims of the bosses and with the way in which the organization should be going. The only thing to do in these cases is to act to change the oral tradition. One way of doing this is to put on a performance, as the C.E.O. did, to convince people that a change in aims had indeed taken place.

Rules and Red Tape

No discussion of rules and reorganization would be complete without some consideration of the problem of red tape. Red tape gets its name from the tape or ribbon that used to tie official papers that were delivered to government officers. The term *red tape* now refers to the unnecessary and confusing busywork that is caused by a swelling number of rules and regulations. Employees may look at a reorganization plan as just more red tape. Yet not all the rules, regulations, and procedures in an organization are considered red tape. This leads us to ask why some rules and regulations are seen as unnecessary busywork and why other rules and regulations are seen as important parts of a job.

One situation that tends to make rules and procedures seem like red tape to the employees occurs when workers feel that their status has been impugned by having their work inspected and checked, as if the administrative officials assumed that all of the employees were incompetent, sloppy, and careless. Any procedure that requires repeated checking and the approval of multiple officials will probably be viewed as unnecessary red tape. Interference, in particular, often amounts to an attack on the employee's sense of worth, for it is regarded as though the official is calling the employee's competence into question. Another circumstance that makes procedures appear to be red tape is the power-power conflict that occurs when the officials who interpret the rules are out of reach of the people who are expected to obey the rules, so that it becomes almost impossible to get approval for making exceptions to the rule. In such a situation the rule tends to be followed grudgingly by the people involved. The employees become resentful because they feel powerless to do their job properly.

Finally, any procedure that seems unnecessarily complex and confusing is called "red tape." When everything must be filled out in ten copies or when the same information must be copied down in

ten different places, employees tend to feel that this is an unnecessary burden and complain that they do not see why two or three
people can't share the same information that is collected. In many
cases, they are right. Any reorganization that is perceived by the
employees as just more red tape is doomed to failure before it is
started. The creation of new rules as a form of reorganization must
be truly necessary for the organization, and the rules should be applied in such a way that employees feel they are doing their jobs well
in following the new rules and procedures.

JOB REDESIGN

The design and redesign of jobs has been going on, historically, since
the decline of the independent craftsman and the rise of factory production. For over 200 years the tendency had been to design jobs in
such a way that they were "idiot proof." The idiot-proof job was
supposed to be one in which the task was so simple and routine that
it could be done accurately by any intelligent ape. This trend in job
design had the unfortunate side effects of making workers feel as
though they were idiots to do the job; in other words, it deprived
them of any job-connected source of worth. As a consequence of
this, industries found themselves with high rates of absenteeism and
poor production quality as a result of the chronic boredom created
by these highly simplified jobs. The more recent trend in job redesign and job enrichment has been to try to counter the unpleasant
side effects caused by the trend toward idiot-proof jobs.

   In the previous discussion on feedback, the delegation of
authority, and organizational rules and red tape, we have touched on
some of the problems involved in job redesign in the context of the
entire organization. For instance, in discussing the delegation of
authority, we noted that if the delegation of authority does not
change a single aspect of the task to be done by workers, it still
changes their feelings about the job and about the responsibilities
they have in working effectively without close supervision. In terms
of feedback in organizations there has been an information revolution. Information that was too expensive to collect and process when
it was done by an army of clerks in an office is now easily and
cheaply available on the daily computer printout. The feedback pro-

cess has been greatly enhanced by the availability of cheap, up-to-date information about the workings of the organization. Job performance can be monitored indirectly, and this allows jobs to be designed more around the problems of doing the task than around the problems of direct supervision. Tasks no longer have to be done in the context of an organizational hierarchy designed for direct supervision and coordination. Information feedback systems have eliminated much of the necessity for the old organizational hierarchy and have made new organizational designs possible. Finally, it should be clear from our previous discussion about organizational rules that such rules are the building blocks of business and government organizations. Job redesign will succeed or fail depending on how people interpret and use the new rules. Although our knowledge and understanding of the problems of job redesign have increased greatly in the last ten years, there are still some problems that we need to be wary of when we are thinking about reorganizing a company.

Forms of Redesign

Let's look at what has served as the basis of job redesign in the past. Jobs are seen as being made up of specific tasks, which can be clearly defined and which take a set amount of time to perform before they are repeated. This amount of time is called the job cycle. Tasks may be combined to form a specific job. In general, the methods of job redesign have assumed a one person–one task unit of organization; thus, the analysis that goes into job redesign has been weighted heavily toward the individual level of behavior and performance rather than toward the organizational level.

One form of job redesign is to set up a process of *job rotation*, in which workers work at one set of tasks for a period of time and then trade with other workers to do other tasks. Job rotation is seen as a way of relieving boredom and giving some variety to the total work experience. In some cases this works very well, but in other cases the individual may be thrown into a conflict of interests. For example, suppose you rotated the job of production worker with the job of production inspector so that the same individual would work for a while in production and then be expected to act as the inspector for his fellow production workers' output. This kind of job rotation would probably quickly teach management that they cannot let the fox guard the chicken coop.

Experiments have been done with *job enrichment*, in which workers are given an increase in discretion about how they do their jobs, and in which jobs have been made more complex rather than simplified. In many cases it has worked to have workers inspect the quality of their own work in small groups called "quality circles." Using job enrichment programs as a means of job redesign, however, can create stress and conflict with first-level line supervisors, who may feel that their authority has been undermined and that their control over the work situation has been diminished, because the individual workers are now more responsible for planning and executing their jobs.

Finally, *job enlargement* has been tried as a form of job redesign in which the number of tasks that make up a single job is increased. Workers often become annoyed with job enlargement, unless they are part of the planning process itself, because they feel that they are just being asked to do more work for the same amount of money. Many aspects of job redesign succeed or fail depending on who gets to design the job: management or the workers. When the workers are allowed to decide or participate in the decisions regarding job redesign, the management tends to feel that their authority to run things the way they see fit is threatened. Unless the company is prepared to let the workers do their own planning and does not meddle in the outcome of that planning, then job enlargement programs can produce considerable labor-management conflict.

Problems of Redesign

One of the problems that is often overlooked in the area of job redesign is that a job consists of a group of tasks that are performed in the context of the organization as a whole. Therefore, people's expectations for other people's behavior and for their own behavior must be made clear, so that the wrong expectations won't develop. Some expectations *will* develop: Individuals will assign to any set of tasks a particular status or importance in the organization whether the organization assigns that or not.

Unfortunately, jobs are often designed in such a way that they do not create realistic combinations of expectations, or roles, for the people to play. For a moment, let's look at the problem of job redesign the way others have seen it in the past, as simply the combining of tasks and the assigning of these tasks to individuals. Now let's imagine that we create the job of vice-president for marketing and sales and give to the new vice-president responsibility for overseeing the sales force and its operation, as well as for overseeing the advertising and packaging of the products. Because this new vice-president will no doubt be staying in the building late, let us also add to the list of responsibilities the task of cleaning the bathrooms. Obviously, the combination of tasks given to this vice-president is absurd; yet there are numerous industrial examples in which tasks as varied and uneven in status as these have been combined into one job. The point here is that the combining of tasks into a job does not necessarily create a work role that can realistically be performed by an individual in the context of the organization.

Another problem with job redesign is that jobs are created out of a set of prescribed tasks. These are usually tasks directly related to production or information processing, but the effective performance of a job usually requires that the individual also perform discretionary tasks. If the discretionary tasks are not allowed for in planning a job, or if the individual feels that it is not part of his or her responsibility to perform these tasks, the result may be the complete breakdown of the work operation. This is particularly true when machine operators in a production line do not consider minor maintenance their responsibility or do not consider the reporting of serious maintenance problems part of their job. Without these discretionary tasks being performed, machine downtime can become a major problem. The reorganization efforts within a company that include job redesign must take into account that social roles are being formed as well as jobs and that these jobs have discretionary tasks that go along with the prescribed tasks that are used in the planning. It is also important that the redesigned job can be evaluated in terms of some standard of accountability in which supervisors and workers will know that they can rely on these tasks being done correctly. All of this requires a fairly high level of cooperation on the part of workers and supervisors. Thus, when these conflicts have been going on for a long period of time, job redesign itself does not always become a viable solution to organizational conflicts, unless considerable preparatory work of the kind described in Chapter 9 is done.

When a company is plagued with conflict and reorganization seems called for, it is important to remember that all plans have their flaws and that these flaws may create more, not less, conflict. The biggest pitfall in any organization plan is not accepting the realistic limits of the various methods that are used in reorganization. If careful attention is paid to the context in which work is being done and to the participational needs of individuals in the context, then many of the shortcomings of reorganization plans can be anticipated. The delegation of authority requires the genuine transfer of both power and responsibility and at the same time the acceptance of both power and responsibility by the workers. This aspect of reorganization is never easy to achieve and may take a tremendous amount of time. Reorganization based on improved feedback systems cannot be made failsafe. Where information feedback is involved there are always different interpretations of the same information. Making up new rules is also not a failsafe method of accomplishing organizational ends. The new rules may create resentment or additional problems that defeat their purposes.

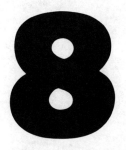

CHANGING
THE STRUCTURE

When we consider changing the structure of an organization we are not talking about changing people but about changing the framework in which people interact and do their jobs. The hope is that with this approach the people themselves will change and acquire new attitudes about their work and face new problems in a cooperative manner. One of the reasons that job redesign has had such popularity as an approach to problems of conflict and inefficiency in organizations is that often it is easier to change the structure than to change the people and leave the old structure intact. Human beings are to a great extent creatures of their environment, so if we change their environment by changing the structure of the patterns of human relationships in that environment, then we have a good chance of creating a better organization.

Changing the structure of an organization may be the only solution to persistent conflicts. When reassignments of personnel or role clarification discussions fail to eliminate conflict, it may be because the conflicts are a part of the structure itself. Organizations, with their many interconnected relationships, can create stresses and strains that can go undiagnosed for some time. Organizations must continue to change as they take on new functions, as economic conditions change, or as their relationship to the community changes. Sometimes these changes are for the good of the organization, and sometimes these changes go unnoticed but create persistent stresses and strains in the old organizational structures. We have discussed in earlier chapters many of the kinds of stresses and strains whose cause can be located in the structure of relationships themselves. In many of these cases we have suggested simple adjustments or reforms in the work relationship to eliminate the causes of these conflicts.

In this chapter we are going to look at the structure in greater detail and ask you to take a highly objective and pragmatic point of view towards the problem of changing organizational structure. The problem of changing the structure, like the "worst case scenario" developed by strategic planners, forces the manager to accept nothing as sacred or immutable and to assume that everything can be done differently, if necessary. When we are changing an organizational structure we are changing how the game is played by rewriting the game's rule book. Because structures are interconnected, we must evaluate possible changes in light of consequences throughout the organization. Major changes have such far-reaching consequences within the organization that carrying them out may require reorganization of other large units or of the company as a whole.

Restructuring an organization is a massive change, and it represents one of the most drastic measures we can take to eliminate conflict. For this reason, restructuring requires the use of much organizational power as well as a considerable amount of cooperation from many of the employees in the organization. The creation of a smoother-running organization must be a high priority goal for many of the members of the organization or else the restructuring will not take hold.

WHAT'S IN A JOB?

The most elementary unit of structural change consists of changing the jobs that people do. The job is the point where the individual and the organizational structure come together. To a great extent it is the job that gives individuals power, that makes demands upon individuals, and that creates the feelings of worth that can produce either conflict or cooperation.

To begin with, let's analyze what's in a job. If we are going to restructure an organization, we must have an idea of what the basic components of a job are so that we can see what our restructuring options will be.

A job consists of two important elements. The first element is a "task" or tasks that we assign to individuals to do. The second element, whose importance becomes clear when we realize that a job is also a position in the organization, is "status." Each job has a definite status, and each individual brings his or her own background status to his or her job. The elements of task and status cannot be separated in the real world. Nevertheless, different management philosophies have tended to emphasize task at the expense of status or vice versa. This has been one of the major shortcomings of attempts to change organizational structures.

TURNING TASKS AROUND

Tasks make up a job structure and define the use of time in a work place. Employees are expected to do tasks over time in a given place. All of this gives a very clear and specific picture of what the job consists of. In reality, the tasks that make up a job are not always easily defined. Some jobs are defined rather tightly, where the employees know exactly what tasks they are expected to do, and other jobs are defined rather loosely, so that it is not clear exactly what is called for, which means that the employees must decide how they are going to do the job. Defining the tasks that make up a job, either tightly or loosely, has both benefits and shortcomings. If a job is defined tightly, then the employees know exactly what is expected of them and they avoid the problem of ambiguity about what the job consists of. This can also mean that the job becomes boring and repetitive and that it varies little from week to week and year to year. Jobs whose tasks are defined loosely, however, present problems of ambiguity about who is supposed to do what, when, and why. Employees who satisfactorily solve this problem of ambiguity may develop a strong sense of satisfaction and self-worth in doing their jobs their own way. The flexibility that an organization gains from having its jobs defined loosely in terms of tasks can often be accomplished by a job-orientation program for new employees that emphasizes that they are expected to do what needs to be done as it needs to be done.

Many jobs are defined in terms of their "prescribed tasks." The tendency is to plan the work structure around these prescribed tasks as if they were simple parts to a puzzle. Yet, if an organization is to operate effectively, the employees need to feel that they are expected to exercise their own discretion to keep things operating smoothly. It is difficult to write down on paper all of the "discretionary tasks" that are included in any ordinary job. Nevertheless, the job cannot be adequately performed unless the employee does both the prescribed and the discretionary tasks. It is well known that employees do not exercise discretion unless they feel that their supervisor and other employees will grant that they are doing their job the best way that they know how. Discretion is one of the first things that is eliminated when management sets up a system of close, punitive supervision. It is important, then, in defining a job, to find a set of complementary tasks that an individual can do without too much interference but also without having to be isolated. You will not create an effective, conflict-free design by setting up a set of tasks that isolates each worker. Tasks should always be interconnected so that doing a job requires some level of teamwork.

Procedures for task and time scheduling have been well worked out in such systematic methods as Critical Path Models (CPM) and Program Evaluation and Review Techniques (PERT). These programs emphasize the time scheduling of work outcome or "milestones," and they feature methods of breaking down all of the components for completing a major project and methods of assigning time and manpower resources to the completion of the schedule. They are useful methods, as long as we keep in mind the shortcomings of this kind of task planning. One shortcoming of these methods is the system of evaluation that is used to keep a project on schedule. Evaluation procedures are an important force in defining jobs for people. An evaluation procedure can stress the quality of activities that the person is engaged in, or it can stress just the outcome of the task. Stress on outcome alone was what led to the absurd situation in which a Soviet factory manager was praised for increasing his production of radios by 200 percent—though only one radio in ten actually worked. If a conscious effort is not made to keep track of the actual activities or skills that go into a job, then problems of stress caused by work overload, high work demands, and a reduced sense of worth can become serious problems created by the structure.

When taking a system of tasks and making them into jobs, keep in mind that human beings, not robots, are going to do these jobs. Different levels of organizational integration can be achieved by building into the system of tasks, where feasible, a certain amount of redundancy and by creating overlapping linkages by assigning the same task to different jobs. When these things are clearly spelled out, and cooperative agreements between the individuals are worked out, a system of complex tasks can be accomplished without creating too much stress.

One of the keys to creating a high level of organizational integration is the information flow. The more that each worker knows about the operations of that unit, the easier it will be to maintain cooperation. In addition, the more that subordinates know about the overall operation of the unit, the less supervision they will need. In an ideal situation, tasks should coordinate themselves so that once the workers have learned their jobs, direct supervision will not be necessary. Supervisors should be seen as problem solvers and not as people who maintain order and routine. The coordination of task performances in an organization has to be evaluated in terms of the problems of power, work demands, and feelings of worth. The task design can have profound effects upon the quality of work performance.

Five Tips on Tasks

It often seems that if you have to do everything at once, then you can't do anything at all. The assignment, scheduling, and coordination of tasks is critical to the reduction of conflict in organizations. The following five rules are helpful for the process of restructuring the work of organizations:

1. Combine related tasks so that they can be completed by the same worker or group of workers in the same time unit. This principle regulates work demand and promotes a sense of worth by allowing workers to complete as much of a project as possible before going on to other tasks.
2. Workers or groups of workers with complementary tasks need to be able to interact freely so as to establish their own coordi-

nation. This principle tends to reduce the friction caused by poorly coordinated work demands.

3. If a worker or group of workers must perform several different and unrelated tasks, then make sure that each task has a separate time scheduled for it. Also, make sure that you allow for a clean break between one work demand and another so that the people or group of persons can shift gears. This tends to reduce the conflicts caused by competing work demands.

4. When evaluating task performance, stress the quality of the performance as much as the quantity of the output. When this rule is followed it tends to reinforce the sense of self-worth that workers have in their jobs.

5. The supervision and evaluation of task performance should be done by those closest to the performance of the task. This should be done by the first-line supervisor or by the workers themselves. When this principle is followed it tends to keep power and responsibility from becoming separated.

These five rules for restructuring tasks should be seen as "rules of thumb" that can help in locating conflict caused by poor task assignment or that can help in job redesign.

JOBS AND THE PERSONAL STATUS STRUCTURE

The status structure of an organization is probably the most important aspect to look at in trying to solve problems of conflict. Jobs are not just tasks; they represent positions in an organization, and these positions have a definite status or importance. Status considerations are often more of an obstacle to solving conflicts than are characteristics of the tasks, because status affects how a person is regarded by others and how a person regards his or her job; and these things bear on one's feelings of worth.

People have many statuses (social attributes) that influence their lives, such as their age, sex, race or ethnicity, religion, and organizational memberships. All of these statuses can influence a person's job performance and expectations for a career in the company. Because we cannot change many of these statuses and cannot choose exactly the combination of statuses that we want a person to have, we must focus our attention on the statuses that are created or influenced by personnel policies and the structure of the work organization; we have some control over those statuses.

Many of the statuses that are created out of personnel policies and the structure of the work organization are common to almost every work setting. By focusing on nine of these status elements we will be able to illustrate most of the problems emerging from the status structure of jobs.

Education

The amount of education or formal training that people have influences how they do their jobs and how other people regard their job performance. In the past we generally believed that the more education people had, the better qualified they were to do almost any job, and therefore education was seen as a springboard to getting a good job. In recent years we have seen some changes in attitude toward the importance of education for job qualification. At a time when we can observe people with Ph.D.'s driving taxi cabs, we are beginning to think that there may be such a thing as being overeducated. We have assumed that people will not be satisfied unless they are doing a job that calls for the level of education that they have. To some extent this is true. Yet what a number of employers have found is that the opposite rule of thumb is also true. If you give people jobs for which they lack the necessary educational credentials, they will work hard trying to prove themselves and will gain a great deal of satisfaction from the job. A manager's confidence that a person can perform in a job can be an important source of feelings of worth for the individual.

Some of the problems that formal education causes in the status structure of an organization stem from the fact that emphasis is given to education, rather than performance, so that people are regarded as better or more valuable employees simply because they have more education rather than because they get their jobs done and work well with others. A person's level of education should never be allowed to substitute for performance. This is true even when a high level of education is called for, as with engineers or computer experts. Nevertheless, education does set up a certain expectation as to how a person should perform (after all, employees with masters degrees are expected to act like they know something), and these expectations can get in the way of job performance when highly educated people have to deal with people who lack a strong educational background—

particularly when the people with less educational background have the experience to do the job well. Therefore, when assigning people with different levels of education to different job tasks, you should try to strike a balance between those with education and those with experience. The educational expectations and the performance demands should enhance an individual's feelings of worth and job satisfaction, not hinder job performance.

Prior Job History

We have all read job advertisements where the last line reads "experience required." We have all felt the annoying absurdity of being told that to get a job you must have experience, and have said to ourselves, "How can I get experience if I can't get the job?" An employee's background represents an accumulation of skills and statuses that he brings to the job. Some of these background experiences represent what the employee may feel are reasonable demands that can be made upon him and some may represent what he may feel are unjust demands. In the same sense, his feelings of worth may be greatly influenced by the fact that a new job offers him more freedom, more flexibility in his working hours, or the feeling that the new job is a step up in his career. By hiring people who do not have direct experience in the job that you are creating you have an advantage: You can train them yourself to fit the job, and you can set the new work expectations without having to worry about their past experience. The disadvantage of this is that this training takes time. Many employers, however, do not seem to appreciate that many of the skills that their employees use in their jobs are skills that are necessary to do many other jobs. There are many jobs that require people who can be at ease in meeting people and who can make a good impression, jobs that require people who can work with budget figures and who can pay attention to detail, and so on. By realizing what skills you are looking for, you will find that you have a large number of potential applicants to pick from if you are willing to do a little retraining yourself.

Timing in Career

Most organizations expect that jobs that require a certain level of responsibility and command a certain level of salary should be given to employees whose age and experience warrant those positions. We have all seen articles about individuals who become presidents of major corporations at age twenty-five, and the reason this is newsworthy is because, impressed as we are, unconsciously we feel that this is too young for a person to peak in his or her career. Within some broad limits we generally agree that the positions that call for supervising others or the positions that carry with them a great deal of responsibility should be given to older and more-experienced employees. It may be a mistake to put a young, inexperienced employee in a job that is a supervisory position or that is seen by others in the organization as a position of great responsibility, because others won't take the person seriously or will feel resentment and will try to "cut 'em down to size." On the other hand, older and more-experienced employees may feel that they naturally deserve a particular job that becomes available and, when they get it, they may not feel that they need to perform at as high a level as the less-experienced employee would. At either extreme there are problems of career timing. In most cases, however, simply recognizing these problems makes it easy to avoid the pitfalls.

Duration in Job

How long a person has done a job influences his or her attitude about the job and influences how people relate to the person. Experience in a job can create self-confidence, a sense of worth, and feelings of importance because other, less-experienced employees turn to that person for advice and help. There is no substitute for knowing what you are doing and being comfortable about doing it. Yet, while these are the things we value about experience, duration in a job can have its drawbacks. The longer someone does a job, the more likely the person is to feel that he or she deserves some special privileges or extra recognition, say in the form of higher pay. It is not surprising, therefore, to find in many studies that the more-experienced workers are also the ones who have the highest job dissatisfaction. Consciously or unconsciously, workers feel that the company owes them something for their years of good service, and to some extent it does. In addition, workers with considerable experience in a job are often the ones who are most reluctant to adjust to a new system of work organization, because their status is based on the old system. Changes can be made, however, if a person's duration in the job is respected when the new job assignments are made, so that the person doesn't feel that he or she is being "put out to pasture."

Expectations for Promotion

We often find that a person's attitudes towards the job and his or her performance in the job have nothing to do with that job at all, but instead have to do with the person's belief that if the job is done well, he or she will have a good chance for promotion to a new job. At the same time a person's feelings of worthlessness or feeling that the job demands are too great may come from the feeling of being trapped in the job and the fear of never getting promoted. However, a person's expectations for promotion may not correspond to his real chances for promotion. His expectations will be based, in large part, on his interpretation of what happens to others in the organization. These expectations may be extremely important, because they often affect the work performance of the employee.

For example, a company may decide that an outsider should be brought in to fill a vacant position because the insiders, the employees in the unit, have formed too many ties of loyalty to others in the unit to supervise without favoritism. The employees may interpret this decision as a sign that the company won't reward hard work by promotion. Indeed, the employees may feel so much resentment over the decision that they will ensure that the outsider fails.

Similar problems arise when organizations have made changes in their structure. When an organization is restructured, many of the old expectations of promotion are no longer valid; so the first few promotions made under the new design are critical for forming the new expectations as to which jobs are steppingstones to better jobs. A person who is in a job that is regarded as a steppingstone to a better job has a different status than a person who is in a job that is regarded as a dead-end job. By making particular promotion decisions a manager may inadvertently change what had been considered to be a steppingstone into a dead-end job, thus changing the status of the employee in that job. This may have serious consequences for the organization, in terms of the work performance of that employee and of others who are trying to gauge their own chances for promotion.

Skill Level

A person with a job calling for specialized skills holds a position that can't readily be taken over by other people, and this affects his or her status in the organization. People who do skilled jobs have a certain amount of power in an organization; they can withhold cooperation with others to get what they want. For this reason companies have often redesigned jobs with greatly reduced skill levels so that anyone can do them with very little training. Yet the skill level of the job has a profound influence over a person's feelings of worth and his or her status in the organization. It is usually necessary to construct jobs with a high enough level of skill that the people doing them will feel that the jobs are worth doing. Skilled work takes on a status of its own, so that people who supervise skilled workers usually have to be recognized as having mastered those skills themselves, or the skilled workers will not feel that the supervisor has the right to tell them what to do. If an organization is changed in a way that creates new skilled jobs, or that changes the circumstances of skilled workers, special care must be taken to ensure that the supervisors can gain the respect of the workers. If under the new structuring of an organization the skilled workers feel neglected, demoted, or unfairly dealt with, they can cause a great deal of conflict because they control certain tasks. Generally, people with specialized skills expect special treatment in the sense that they do not expect to be treated the same way lesser skilled workers are treated. So when you redesign the structure, you must treat skill levels not merely as a job position but also as a status.

Responsibility

Some jobs carry with them greater responsibility than others, and therefore people expect a greater amount of respect and consideration for accepting this responsibility. Yet responsibility is often assigned only to a particular job; even though people in other jobs do the same tasks, they do not bear the responsibility. Let's use as an example the status difference between a pilot and a copilot on a commercial airliner. Both the pilot and the copilot are capable of performing the same tasks that are necessary for flying the airplane, and both of them may have extensive experience and thus may be equally capable of doing the job. Nevertheless, the pilot is paid substantially more money for doing the same tasks that the copilot can do because he has been designated as having responsibility for the operation of the aircraft. If something goes wrong, the pilot is blamed for it, and this is primarily what is meant by responsibility.

You cannot always tell what the pattern of responsibility in an organization is just by asking people. Ask people instead, "Who is likely to be blamed if something goes wrong?" The answer to that question will begin to identify the real pattern of responsibility. Because the pattern of responsibility is sometimes obscure, people are not always recognized and rewarded for the responsibility that they carry. Supervisors can often blame their workers for mistakes, making their workers carry the burden of responsibility. When this happens, it is predictable what the feelings of the workers will be when they find out that they must absorb all the blame. In redesigning the jobs in an organization you can avoid worker resentment by making sure that responsibility is clearly defined and rewarded and that the criticism and blame get directed to the people in those positions.

Position in a Job Network

Some positions in a job network become more important and influential simply because the people in them have access to an enormous amount of information, or because a large number of other workers depend upon those people to do their job correctly. So a person's position in the job network can enhance his or her informal status simply because of the design of the network. Job networks can also produce problems, however, by isolating workers so that they are separated from the work of other people and from necessary information. This kind of isolation is often unintentionally created around middle-echelon supervisors who are not involved in the work that their employees are doing and may not be involved in the information communication processes of the organization as a whole. People in this situation are often heard complaining, "Why don't people tell me what's going on around here?" If a supervisor decides to correct this problem by insisting that the workers fill out more forms and report every detail of their work, the supervisor only makes matters worse by increasing the work demands and undermining the employees' sense of worth by signalling to them that the supervisor questions their ability to do their jobs.

What is important to recognize here is that regardless of the nature of the job being done, the way in which the job is arranged and organized and the way in which people are involved with each other in work relationships produce a system of statuses. These status differences have important consequences for the level of cooperation or conflict that is created. If a key position is created by the information and task flow of a work unit, then it might be beneficial to formalize communication between that position and the supervisor by making the person with that job an assistant to the supervisor; in that way the supervisor can be kept informed about the problems of the unit.

Salary Level

The level of salaries and wages can be the focal point of more dissatisfaction, griping, and conflict than probably any other aspect of an organization, because it is through differences in salaries or wages that we indicate differences in status and worth. A salary is more than just a living wage. It is a symbol of the status that a particular person has in the organization. Consider, for example, the salaries of executives. We might say that an executive who makes $300,000 dollars a year could live just as well if he or she made $250,000 dollars a year. And we might be hard pressed to defend the idea that his or her contribution to the organization was a hundred times greater than some hourly employee. Nevertheless, he or she is paid that amount of money partly because, as an executive, it is expected that he or she be among the highest paid people in the organization. Assigning pay levels to an individual who has a unique combination of statuses seems like an almost impossible task, yet the job can be made a little easier if we pay attention to statuses rather than task performance. When people decide that they are not being paid what they are worth, it is often on the basis of how they compare themselves to other people. When people feel that their value to the organization—that is, their status—is not recognized, they often become highly sensitive to the fact that other people with lower status in the organization are doing as well as or better than they are. When you begin redesigning a structure, and you decide how you are going to acknowledge certain statuses such as education or duration in the job, you will find that pay levels are one method you can use to make these distinctions important to people. By setting pay levels, you are saying that certain people are regarded as equals in the organization, because they make approximately the same amount of money, and that other people are superior or subordinate in the organization, because they make relatively more or less money. Thus, you can use pay levels to smooth out some of the old status differences and establish new ones. If you are starting from scratch with a new structure, it helps if you can keep the pay differences reasonably small, and at the same time make people feel that their work is being recognized in their level of pay.

These nine status dimensions are a part of the status structure of jobs in an organization, and their capacity for causing conflict should never be underestimated.

CHARTING A NEW STRUCTURE

Creating a new structure requires that we be able to put the tasks that need to be done together with the statuses of the people who will do them; we should do this in such a way that there will be a minimum of conflict-producing situations. Table 8-1 lists the key elements to be contended with in constructing a design.

TABLE 8-1. Construction of a Job Design.

Task Structure	Personal Status Structure
a. Prescribed tasks	1. Education
1. Loosely defined	2. Prior job history
2. Tightly defined	3. Timing in career
b. Discretionary tasks	4. Duration in job
1. Work atmosphere	5. Chances of promotion
2. Style of supervision	6. Skill level
c. Evaluation of	7. Responsibility
1. Work activity or skill	8. Position in job network
2. Outcomes (productivity)	9. Salary level

Once you have identified all the tasks that must be done in a section of the company and have laid them out on a type of flow chart so that they can be combined into interrelated jobs, then check to make sure that you have included all the jobs that will be assigned. Be sure that supervision, evaluation, and inspection tasks are included as well as the primary work tasks. It is important to include every function from your list of tasks that you have combined into jobs, because you are trying to create as complete a picture of the work that needs to be done as possible.

After you have constructed the list of jobs, you need to assign to certain jobs those statuses that deal with skill level, responsibility, and position in the job network. If this position is determined by the work flow, then it is important to make up a list of the employees who will do these jobs and, in a simple shorthand form, list after each employee's name his or her relative statuses, or potential status expectations. With these two lists and a fresh pad of paper, combine the two lists to form the new structural design. You may adapt the Job and Status Structure Planning Sheet in the appendix. To aid you in this project, we have given you some principles that will help you foresee problems as you reorganize. These principles will not solve all of your problems, but they will keep you on track as you assign tasks to people with various statuses.

The Principle of Equals

The principle of equals means that the same tasks should be performed by people of approximately the same set of statuses. If for the same task there is approximately the same level of responsibility, skill, education, chance for promotion, and approximately the same salary level for everyone doing that task, then cooperation is easier to obtain and there are fewer hard feelings. When people doing the same task have vastly different statuses, those who are short changed will feel resentment, which can produce dissension and conflict.

The Principle of Differences

When jobs involve a hierarchy of different responsibilities or skill levels, the social statuses of the people doing those jobs should reflect those differences. To apply the principle of differences, you look at not only the education and skill level of employees but also at their prior job history, the timing in their careers, their chances of promotion, as well as salary level. Statuses should be matched with jobs in such a way that employees feel that their worth is respected by the job structure. In particular, employees with jobs lower in the hierarchy should feel that people in higher positions deserve their positions of higher status. The principle of differences, simply put, refers to the fact that where differences occur in the task structure, these differences should also be reflected in the status structure.

The Principle of Nonreversals

The principle of nonreversals is that the work flow should not create a situation in which high status employees find themselves in a position where they must take orders from, or become dependent on, lower status employees. This situation tends to create serious conflicts. In a case of reversal, real power moves in the opposite direction from expected power, so that the high status person is being told what to do, or is totally at the mercy of a lower status employee. Such a situation can be created when there is a difference in responsibility, skill level, or position in the job network, so that the lower status employee can exercise informal power in the relationship. In status reversals the principle of differences is violated; because it produces complaining, hypersensitivity, and power conflicts, it deserves special consideration. When task flows demand that certain power reversals occur in the work structure, they can sometimes be stabilized by formalizing the communication between the two jobs, so that the two people communicate with each other only through memos or written forms, rather than in face-to-face interaction. This formalization of intereaction can reduce the status threat created by a power reversal.

The Principle of Linkage

Many times it is impossible to set up a work flow so that two groups or two individuals will not become a source of conflict. Sometimes power reversals, competitive situations, or power-demand problems are likely to occur. In these cases, you should have the two groups or individuals deal with each other through some third person, or mediator. This person's position is a position of linkage between two potentially conflicting job status groups. Linkages can take two forms. The first is a form in which an individual is assigned as a mediator to communicate and coordinate the demands of each side. In this case, the mediator must have limited formal responsibility but a significant status in the eyes of each group. This form of linkage represents one solution to the problem of power reversals. A second form of linkage occurs when two very diverse groups must interact in the organization, in which case you need to put two people in the linking position. This form of linkage often occurs in underdeveloped nations where the management of a company is of one ethnic background, and the laborers in the company are of another ethnic background. In this situation it is sometimes necessary to have two people play the role of supervisor so that management has a supervisor from its ethnic group, and the workers have a supervisor from their ethnic group. For this to work, these two individuals must get along. It is easier to get two individuals to get along than it is to get two groups to get along; therefore, it is worthwhile to have two people do the job of supervisor so that compromises at the work site can be easily achieved.

These four principles should serve as initial rules of thumb for setting up a new work structure in a way that avoids conflict. Even if you are not in a position to restructure the entire organization, you can use these concepts in your organization to locate potential sources of conflict, by breaking down the tasks that make up jobs and comparing the status elements that employees bring to the various jobs. A simple analysis following these rules of thumb may turn up the sources of basic conflict, which might be solved by simply shifting some people around from job to job.

REWRITING RULES

The problem of setting up a new system of rules parallels the problem of job restructuring. A system of work rules or personnel rules should not interfere with or break the task flow of the jobs if at all possible, and the system of rules should follow the status line of the new structure. Work rules or personnel rules always apply to specific people in specific situations. Therefore, it is not difficult to apply a rule to people who do approximately the same jobs and have approximately the same statuses. However, specific rules can become the focal point of conflict if they imply that one work group is somehow inferior or has a reduced status relative to some other group. It is more difficult to set up and enforce rules that apply to everyone in the organization. The tendency is for rules that are universal and "apply to everyone" in practice to apply only to the lower status employees, and this can cause a great deal of resentment on the part of those employees. It must be recognized in this situation that the ignoring of a rule by high status employees becomes a symbol of their high status, and therefore a crackdown can be highly resented by the high status employees as an attack on their privileged position. If you must impose universal rules, then it will be necessary for you to solve this status problem. One way of doing this is to grant certain privileges to people with higher status, so that these privileges can serve as the symbols of high status.

In a given group of employees it is not unusual to find that the older workers ignore some of the rules. Their ignoring of the rules becomes a symbol of their status as older employees in the organization. If you have decided that you need for these rules to be followed by all employees, then you may need to devise a system of granting small privileges to workers who have been with the company for some years. These small privileges can then become the symbols of differential status between the older workers and the younger workers. If the privileges are trivial enough, the younger workers won't resent them and the older workers may value them greatly. If you can satisfy the employees' need for some sign of higher status in a simple way, such as allowing these workers to select the color of their telephone, you can be more demanding about having these workers follow particular rules. However, it is not always easy to know why a rule isn't being followed. Some rules, particularly safety rules, get in the way of performing the task. If that is the case, people will usually tell you and will explain how the rule interferes with the task. But if people choose to ignore a rule to show that they have a higher status, they will not give substantive reasons for not following the rule—they will tell you that the rule is silly or foolish or that "nobody else follows it so why should they?"

There is probably no way of creating a new system of rules in the process of reorganization that will not cause some stress or conflict in the new work structure. If, however, you try your best to avoid certain obvious problems and specify as clearly as possible the function of the rule for each group of employees, then after a period of time you will probably be able to readjust and rewrite the rule system to follow the actual performance of the organization under the new structure.

CONCLUSION

Creating a new structure is a radical solution to the problem of conflict. It requires an artful redesigning of jobs so that the problems of task performance and status are resolved. The problems of job demand, worth, and power must be solved by the design in such a way that the new organization will not have the old conflicts. Creating a new organizational structure requires a good deal of study, close attention to detail, and creativity. It also requires a fair amount of luck, for there is no foolproof formula for creating an organization without some conflicts. Yet, restructuring can eliminate the old and costly conflict situations, and with proper feedback and correction, as well as patience, a better design can be turned into a better-operating organization.

**INFORMAL
SOLUTIONS**

Formal solutions to conflicts—new procedures, new methods of evaluation, new arrangements of tasks—are often not feasible or practical. In many large organizations the authority needed to make changes of this sort just is not in the hands of anyone at the appropriate level. In conflict situations in state bureaucracies, for example, even the governor may lack the authority to change the situation. Similarly, in large business organizations, control over the one thing that needs changing, such as an evaluation process, is centered far away from the actual problem. In other organizations, formal solutions may not be feasible because the higher-up who can make the change treats it as a favor for the person who seeks the change, and expects a favor in return. The price of returning this favor may be too high. Other times, when a manager requests a formal change, the upper level management reacts by calling into question the competence of the manager. This is implied in the typical remark, "When so-and-so was in charge down there, he didn't have any problem like that." Consequently *informal* resolutions are often easier to put into effect, and they can achieve the same results if they are properly thought through. However, they may require, in some circumstances, a high degree of skill in handling people.

In this chapter we will discuss three techniques of informal problem resolution: the Organizational Development technique called *team building*, a technique called *role negotiation*, and the technique of using one's power as manager to impose new informal work arrangements.

TEAM BUILDING

In Chapter 6, we discussed the "Catch-22" of organizational change, how reorganization often fails because in order to make the changes that create the coordination, trust, openness, and good lines of communication that is your goal, you need to have this coordination, trust, openness, and these good lines of communication in the first place! Team-building techniques promise to produce these things, and consequently they have been popular methods in Organizational Development practice.

These team-building techniques, which we will describe shortly, can be very valuable when used in conflict situations. The basic premise of team building is that to reach the goal of trust and cooperation, all that is needed is for people to become trusting and cooperative; thus, the problem becomes a matter of transforming attitudes and starting the habit of trust and mutual regard. The basic flaw in this idea is that rarely is this the *only* problem. In conflict situations there are almost always other problems that get in the way of personal relations of trust and mutual regard. What is achieved by team building is often quickly eroded by the workday irritants that have produced the low level of trust and cooperation in the first place.

There are many specific team-building methods, and almost any social occasion in which workers get together away from the usual work pressures can serve for team-building purposes. This can be done more systematically by having the people involved participate in activities that require them to rely on others. In short, they should function as a team so that they can learn both that they must rely on others and that others can rely on them. In one such exercise a group of computer salespeople was brought to a Florida resort. They were a "sales team," in the sense that they all sold computers for the same firm, but they didn't have much contact with one another; indeed, most of them had never met. The group exercises were designed to acquaint them with one another and to establish supportive, trusting relations. Various games were planned for their time at the resort. One was a race between teams of two, which included a canoe-paddling portion, a bicycle-built-for-two portion, and so on. Team building worked here, as it does in many similar cases. Because the computer salespeople learned that they could rely on each other, they could and did call on each other when, for example, a deal needed to be made to supply a company that had computer needs in more than one region. The warm personal feelings and the sense of mutual regard that had been established were enough to make it possible for them to work together.

Ordinarily, team building alone is not enough. In Organizational Development practice there is a name, "re-entry," for the point in a training experience in which the person prepares to take the skill that has been learned or the relationship that has been established and put it into practice in the real workday world. When the relationships started in the team-building experience can be supported and even enhanced by the workplace experiences, as in the case of the cooperating salespeople, then the results stick. Workplace irritants that aren't removed, however, usually prevent the relationships from lasting, and in cases where there is a long history of workplace conflicts, the team-building exercises themselves can turn into disasters that actually make the situation worse. One such case was a university department with a long history of conflicts. A team-building weekend was set up, away from the university, in the charge of a group facilitator who encouraged the participants to relate to one another on a friendly, relaxed basis. Discussions were then held on the department's problems, which were designed to air people's feelings. The results were simple. In the sessions, accusations flew. In the relaxed periods between the sessions, the people in the opposed factions got together to talk about—and get angry about—the things said in the sessions. The ultimate consequence was that the department had to be divided into two units.

This particular case involved deeply held values and personal antagonisms developed during a long period of time. Each side wanted the department run in such a way that the conception of worth that fit with the people in that faction would prevail. In most cases conflicts are not quite this severe, and a team-building effort can be a good first step and a way of avoiding the Catch-22 of organizational change. It cannot be the *only* step. The next step has to be to make the changes in work arrangements that remove the irritants and conflicts.

Removing the irritants and conflicts need not involve formal rule changes. If some of the customs and expectations are changed, this may be enough. Identify the sources of the problems and make the changes that will eliminate them. The methods for identifying and solving problems informally are those outlined in Chapters 4 and 5. Informal changes, however, need to be propped up in various ways. There must be some action, such as mutual promises or public discussion leading to consensus, to which everyone can refer in case of violations. If, for example, it is understood, on the basis of a new agreement, that some particular person in the office has full responsibility for a particular contact task, everyone must know it, agree to it, and make sure that this person gets the phone calls, is fully informed about anything that relates to the contact task, and so on. Sometimes the responsibilities will need to be reaffirmed publicly or to the person who is failing to act in accordance with it.

As with any other change, an informal change should have benefits for everyone affected, and not just for one person, or it will fail. If an assignment is perceived as a "plum" job, or if it appears that the person was given the assignment for the wrong reasons, such as "because the squeaking wheel gets the grease," the agreement will be followed only half-heartedly, if at all. In these cases the assignment undermines the other people's sense of worth—especially their sense that they are not getting the respect they deserve.

ROLE NEGOTIATION

A "tough" alternative to "soft" group techniques such as team building is a method called *role negotiation*. In conflict situations, role negotiation clarifies who is supposed to do what. As with team building, role negotiation is a natural process as well as a technique. Sociologists have studied what they call "negotiated order" in many work settings, particularly in hospitals.

In hospitals the staff performs a wide variety of professional roles, each of which has a particular set of activities that are part of its responsibility. Thus, nurses are clearly in charge of the patients in some situations, but in other situations they are expected to defer to the opinions and judgment of the physicians. In practice, however, these highly general activities may not be very clear. In a life-threatening situation in which it is not possible to get the doctor's opinion, it may nevertheless be necessary for the nurse to act. Although it is usually not the job of the nurse to make explicit diagnostic suggestions, the nurse may notice something that the doctor doesn't. In these situations a body of informal customs emerges. No one writes the rules down; that would be impossible. However, the customs are honored, and they make it possible for everyone to deal with these cases, to know what to expect, and to tell where—more or less—they leave their proper realm of responsibility and go into someone else's.

Role negotiation is a technique that makes this implicit boundary-setting, responsibility-defining activity into an explicit, public exercise. It can be done in various ways, but its primary feature is always that it is an arrangement that is agreed upon by all parties. Accordingly, whatever form the negotiation takes, the process has to assure that the perceptions, desires, attitudes, values, work constraints, and standards of all parties are taken into account.

When there are major differences in status between the parties involved in a conflict, "having a meeting" is not likely to work. The lower status people may feel unable to speak freely or comfortably, and the higher status people may feel that the task of dealing with the lower status people is not properly theirs. The problems here are especially acute when the work situation involves a wide range of professional roles, such as in a hospital.

In general, meetings are ineffective ways of dealing with problems that may be very specific and of no interest to the group as a whole. A better way of handling role negotiation would be to interview the parties of the dispute one by one, and thus bring out the problems. A meeting may be appropriate at the next step. The purpose of this meeting should be to get the parties involved to discuss the problems together. The manager's role should be to structure and monitor the discussion to keep it on the subject of the negotiation of responsibilities and to articulate suggestions.

Despite the drawbacks of meetings, they serve one purpose very well. A meeting in which everyone can see that everyone else is assenting to an arrangement is a good ritual for certifying an agreement and marking a new mutual beginning. Thus, a group meeting is a good last step to a role-negotiation process. Of course, this "last step" is not really the end of the process. Support and monitoring agreements continue to be necessary to reassure everyone that there will be no backsliding.

Here are some basic guidelines for conducting the one-on-one interviews in the role-negotiation process.

1. Use such techniques as "active listening" and paraphrasing to bring out the employee's concerns.
2. Show that you do not "take sides" or "punish," but that you approach the problem in a positive way and are seeking the employee's agreement, rather than criticizing.
3. Ask each employee a) what he or she thinks the other relevant employees need to do more or better in order for the employee to do his or her own job, b) what the other employees need to do less, and c) what the other employees do that increase his or her effectiveness and therefore should continue doing.
4. Depersonalize the messages you convey from one employee to another by focusing on tasks rather than on personal feelings. Don't say, "Joan thinks you are interfering with her schedule," for example. Instead say, "How can we make sure that Joan's schedule is not interfered with, because it decreases her effectiveness?"
5. When an employee tells you something that he or she does not want repeated, respect it. Don't make public something that the employee wants kept private. The result of violating a confidence is that the next time you won't be told!

MANAGER-IMPOSED SOLUTIONS

Role negotiation involves a deal between equals, or people who are acting for the moment as equals. The solution may need the subtle threat or the promise of gratitude and support of the supervisor, but the primary commitments are made between the warring parties. In situations in which "negotiation" is not possible, the manager may intrude considerably more, for example, by saying "negotiate or else," and by defining the solution as well as by enforcing and rewarding the behavior that supports it.

The same principles that govern solutions, discussed in Chapters 4 and 5, govern manager-imposed informal solutions. The difference is that the manager has to be a participant in the solution in a much more active way. Instead of merely getting things on the right track and intervening only to keep things on the right track, the manager must treat the solution as a body of promises and exchanges in which the manager is the central person. Thus, the success or failure of the implementation of the solution depends very heavily on how the manager treats his or her promises.

A frequent feature of conflict situations are the manager's worthless promises. American-style management tends to foster a certain kind of slick, ambitious manager who can put on a good show, generate an atmosphere of intense activity and excitement, and then get out into a better job before it becomes apparent that the whole show had been an unproductive, conflict-breeding, and strictly short-term standoff. The great love of "the bottom line," that is to say quantitative success during a short-range accounting period, makes this kind of manager possible.

One result of this managerial style is that it breeds cynicism. The "good numbers" are often the result of manipulations and tricks, rather than of substantial and tangible improvements. The achievements are often a matter of the manager's skill at self-promotion and selling, rather than of real achievements. The dedicated worker whose sense of worth derives from doing the job well soon recognizes the unreality behind the manager's self-promotion and selling. When this happens, the selling becomes much more difficult, especially within the manager's own unit. Any promises the manager might make at that point will be viewed cynically.

The therapeutic-style manager, the sort who makes a great effort to make everyone "feel good about themselves" as a way of encouraging cooperation, often produces the same results as the self-promoting manager, though in a way that is sometimes more difficult to undo. The manager who plays games with numbers and inflates achievements ultimately undermines his or her own credibility, because the people in the unit know better. The therapeutic manager tries to get changes accepted by manipulating the employees' sense of worth through dishing out universal praise. This kind of manager will tell the employees how good they are, how much he or she values them, and how great a job they are doing. This undermines *everyone's* standards and makes people cynical about all their interactions. The first "stroke" may have a positive influence, and the next twenty may have a positive effect, but the following ten may backfire, especially if the employees realize that they are being manipulated.

Phony praise, no matter how sincerely expressed, ultimately is destructive. There is a deep reason for this. Every work group develops and mutually reinforces work standards that are a basic source of worth for the people in the group. In Chapters 4 and 5 we discussed the question, *With whom does a particular employee check out ideas about work?* This group and its standards are an important source of worth for employees, and when the standards are positive ones, they are often the single most powerful motivating source. If a manager interferes by giving out praise that is contrary to these standards, the praise itself creates a worth-worth conflict, which the workers often will resolve in their own minds by becoming cynical about the manager's praise. Some workers have deeper needs for praise than others, of course, and these workers may become regarded as the "manager's pets" if they succumb to the game of praise and praise seeking.

The therapeutic approach can be most destructive when it works—when people *believe* the constant praise. One manager who took over a new unit decided to follow the general adage that "you can't use too much praise." She told all the employees in the unit how great they were as often as possible. Six months later when asked how it was going, she said, "I've created a monster!" When asked what the matter was, she said, "I kept telling them how great they were at every opportunity, hoping that some of the problems would work themselves out, and now they believe it. The problems still haven't gone away, but now the employees won't accept any criticism because they think they are 'so great.' Their attitude is, 'Who is she to criticize us?' Now what do I do?"

This is not to say that "stroking"—a technique involving giving conscious praise—is always wrong. When a new work arrangement is negotiated, some positive feedback is needed to achieve cooperation, but it should be a matter of the manager's seeing the worth of an employee and telling the truth. But even sincerely felt praise can have drawbacks. For example, if you say to an employee, "I want you to know you're the best employee I've ever had working for me," you are going to create some bad side effects. First, it makes it hard for you to criticize the employee when he or she needs it. Second, the phrase "the best employee I've ever had" sets up an expectation which that employee may not want to live up to. Third, you have implied that the other employees are not very good, and that undermines cooperation. Awards and certain kinds of performance rating may have the same bad effects.

In giving the truthful praise helpful in assuring cooperation, follow this simple rule. Focus the praise on the work, not the person. This means giving praise and encouragement about a specific task, rather than giving general, constant praise. This works more effectively, in the long run, and is better for the employee's sense of worth. Use statements such as

"I like the way you handled that."
"It looks as if you really worked hard on that."
"I need your help on _____, to get it done right."
"It's good to see the progress you're making on _____."

By giving positive feedback in this way, you will be able to maintain your credibility, you will avoid destroying the positive standards that are a source of worth for the employee, and you will motivate the employee to keep doing a good job.

The manager also needs to show respect for the work standards and goals of the organization and the work group. This is a difficult point to grasp, but it is an important one. Again, the analogy to the family is helpful. If you tell your children not to gossip or lie, and then you go ahead and gossip and lie, they will get the message that it's fine to gossip and lie as long as they don't get caught, or they will become cynical about your admonitions.

If you, as a manager, make a promise in exchange for something, you must realize that it is the creation of a standard that you must honor if you expect anyone else to honor promises or expect any promises to be taken seriously. Consequently, you must be very careful to make only those promises that you can keep, promises that people can *see* you are keeping. If you promise to do something that can't be checked out by your subordinates—for example, promise to talk to some higher-up about a raise for those subordinates—you invite doubts about whether you are keeping your side of the bargain if they do not get the raise.

MAKING AN INFORMAL SOLUTION STICK

Once you have settled on an informal solution, you have to present it to the people who need to carry it out. A basic principle here is this: Changes are accepted most readily when they are exchanges. If you go to your employees and say, "From now on, I want you to do such and such," you will be taken as critical, negative, and nonappreciative of the employees' past work. Even if this is in fact the way you feel, this is not the time to express it. Instead, to make an informal solution work, you must set it up so that the employees are doing something in return for something else that you will be doing for them.

It is a principle common to all societies that a gift places a kind of burden on the recipient so that there must be something given in return, even if it is only a piece of paper, such as a thank-you note. In other words, the exchange doesn't need to be equal, but it does need to create an obligation. This is precisely the principle used by salespeople who give you a drink or a small gift in order to sell you something that will gain them a great deal of money. One very successful car salesman declared that when a customer admired his shirt, he would promptly take it off and give it to them! This makes sense only because the gift is obligation-creating.

The "gift" does not have to be large or even material. A sincere compliment recognizing the person's contribution may suffice to create a sense of willingness to do something in return. The gift, however, is often a necessary first step in creating an atmosphere of mutual accommodation and respect. In many cases such things as small raises produce amazing results. A competent but resentful and unhappy worker who feels that no one has recognized a contribution often responds very nicely to a raise. Of course, the raise, or whatever the "gift" is, should not be presented as a deal. The obligation that you want to create is one that goes beyond a short-run deal. The goal, rather, is to build a stronger relationship.

In making changes stick, it is not enough simply to create an obligation to accept the change. The change really has to be better for the people involved, as we have repeatedly pointed out. As a manager you cannot think that your work is done when you've made your subordinates acquiesce. You need to make sure that the informal solution—the new practices—actually work, and you need to take problems seriously and be supportive about them.

The basic form of a manager-imposed informal solution, then, is mutual promises—exchanges—between the manager and each relevant subordinate. Promises must be taken seriously. They must be honored and honored visibly. The processes must also be monitored in an accepting way, one that does not produce more bad information.

CONCLUSION

The methods presented in this chapter are frequently the most simple and effective ways to control a conflict. The solutions are "informal" in the sense that they do not involve changes in the organizational chart, job descriptions, and written procedures, so they do not require as much use of authority—authority that managers often do not have.

Team building is often an essential first step in creating an appropriate atmosphere of mutual regard and trust. The results of team-building exercises will prove fleeting, however, unless the irritants that produce resentment and distrust are removed and better work arrangements are developed. Role negotiation can be a good means of developing the new work arrangements. The "negotiations" provide considerable insight into work problems in the organization, and they can be valuable in clarifying the responsibilities of the people involved and the consequences of their actions.

In other situations, especially those in which there is a low degree of mutual regard, insight, and trust, the manager may need to take a more directive approach. This requires the same kind of reasoning about work situations that we have discussed in this book. Getting employees to adopt the manager's solution requires mutual promises and an exchange between the manager and each employee or unit.

APPENDIX

WORK RELATIONSHIPS OBSERVATION SHEET

Mark the (a) or (b) statements that come closest to fitting your work situation.

1. a. People like to talk to each other. ⎯⎯⎯⎯
    b. People avoid contact with each other. ⎯⎯⎯⎯

2. a. People socialize with one another at lunch or
        outside of work. ⎯⎯⎯⎯
    b. People maintain a strict separation between
        work and their personal lives. ⎯⎯⎯⎯

3. a. People attribute motives of cooperation and
        helpfulness to the actions of others. ⎯⎯⎯⎯
    b. People attribute self-serving motives to the
        actions of others. ⎯⎯⎯⎯

4. a. People joke about themselves and events at work. ⎯⎯⎯⎯
    b. People joke about others in a critical or cruel
        way, or they use sarcastic putdowns. ⎯⎯⎯⎯

5. a. People feel as if they belong and can have a say
        in things. ⎯⎯⎯⎯
    b. People feel as if they are taken for granted. ⎯⎯⎯⎯

6. a. People accept and cooperate with their super-
        visor's requests and instructions. ⎯⎯⎯⎯
    b. People resent their supervisor's requests and
        instructions. ⎯⎯⎯⎯

If you find that you have checked mostly (a) statements and no more than *two* of the (b) statements, you probably do not have a serious conflict problem. If you have checked *three* or more of the (b) statements, however, then you need to start looking for the source(s) of stress and conflict.

Employee _____
(Use one copy for each employee in the conflict situations.)

CONTACT POINTS WITH OTHERS

Names   *Nature of Contact*

a. _____   _____

b. _____   _____

c. _____   _____

d. _____   _____

e. _____   _____

f. _____   _____

Which contact points have positive value for the employee, and what kind? (Transfer letters corresponding to names.)

_____ feels loyalty.

_____ feels achievement.

_____ has friendships.

_____ has a joking relationship.

_____ has a lunching relationship.

_____ other

Which contact points are pressure points for employees, and why? (Transfer letters corresponding to names.)

_____ feels that the job is interfered with by this person.

_____ feels lack of respect for this person.

_____ feels status imbalance (deserves more respect relative to this person).

_____ feels things are dumped on the employee by this person or that overwork results from this contact.

_____ feels this person doesn't understand his/her (employee's) job.

_____ feels this person isn't doing his/her own job properly.

_____ feels this person misuses authority or control.

_____ other

From other pressure point sheets: Which other employees experience this employee as a pressure point, and in what ways?

NAME	DESCRIPTION OF PRESSURE POINT
_____	_____
_____	_____
_____	_____

Employee _____

(Use one copy for each employee in the conflict situation.)

Tasks on job description (prescribed tasks):

_____

_____

_____

_____

How do these tasks bear on the work of other people or units?

_____

_____

_____

_____

Tasks off job description (discretionary tasks: making coffee, United Fund, etc.):

_____

How do these tasks bear on the work of other people or units?

_____

_____

_____

_____

_____

Method of evaluation (annual report by supervisor, etc.):

_____

_____

_____

Form of supervision (Who bosses and how?):

_____

_____

_____

_____

_____

_____

_____

Relation between evaluation and pay raises (Who does which and how do they correspond?):

_____

Pressure point between employee _____ and employee(s) _____ . (Identify pressure point, using names from worksheet 1. Use one sheet for each pressure point.)

Rules and Practices in Connection with Pressure Point Relations

Formal: _____

_____

_____

_____

_____

_____

Informal: _____

_____

_____

_____

_____

_____

Nature of Controlling and Depending Relations at the Pressure Point

_____

_____

_____

_____

_____

_____

Pressure point between employee _____ and employee(s) _____ .

Contact Changes

Can you route around the pressure points?

Can you put a layer (that is, a linking position) between the contact points by routinization or depersonalization?

Can you assign someone else the contact task?

Control-Relationship Changes

Can you control the work pace or flow by a new formal or informal procedure?

Can you change reporting relationships?

Can you change supervision practices?

Can you change control relationships by changing task assignments?

A. Worth-Worth Mismatches

1. Who do employees check with about questions that they have dealing with the correctness or validity of the job or decision?

2. What are the relationships of loyalty? What aspects of the job are employees reluctant to talk about with outsiders—for example, information concealing, evaluation, altering decision of supervisors, etc.?

3. What relations of favoritism operate in the work situation? How do others cope with these relations?

4. What are the "visible signs" of the organization's satisfaction with or valuing of an employee? Do the signs mean something; that is, do they reflect genuine differences? Or are the signs, such as merit pay increases, difficult to interpret and understand as signs of the employee's value? If they are difficult to interpret, how does an employee come to an interpretation? Does he ask peers? Which ones? Is there an organizational folklore that provides an interpretation? Does it nullify the effect of the sign? For example, does getting a better raise in pay simply mean you are a "sucker"?

5. Are employees heavily relying on alternative, nonorganizational sources of worth?

B. Power-Power Conflicts

1. Does the power of a manager or a unit interfere with the work of subordinates?

2. Does the manager or unit have so much power that bad decisions aren't resisted by subordinates or other units and managers?

3. What is the degree to which the manager or unit understands the problems of subordinates or other units? In what ways could power relations be changed to *force* them to become more understanding?

4. Is there a "flunky" attitude toward certain managers? Which managers like to have "real" followers and lots of flattery? Which have a "macho" style, and who encourages this style?

5. What happens when a task is delegated and doesn't go well? Is it handled with understanding, or is it handled punitively and judgmentally?

6. Does the power of a manager lead to distortions in the information received from subordinates?

7. Does the power of a manager enable and/or encourage concealing or distorting the information the manager gives to superiors and others who "need to know"?

C. Organizational Demand-
Organizational Demand Conflicts

1. Does one assignment interfere with another assignment? Can these conflicts usually be managed, sometimes be managed, or only rarely be managed?

2. Are there informal expectations that make demands that conflict? Are there elements of the folklore of the organization that the employee treats as things that need to be done (for example, to protect oneself) and that conflict with other organizational demands?

3. Can the employee manage the conflict on his or her own, or does it require the cooperation, approval, or understanding of several superiors?

4. How does the evaluation process aggravate the conflict?

5. Does the employee have worth problems because of the conflict? How does he or she resolve the worth problems? How does the employee think about the situation in order to cope with the way it reflects on self-worth?

D. Organizational Demand-Worth Conflicts

1. Which assignments in the organization are considered demeaning?

2. What does a worker or manager need to do to get the respect, trust, or friendship of peers? Do these things conflict with assigned tasks?

3. Are there situations in which a worker or manager has to harm another worker or manager to fulfill the demands placed on him or her by the organization?

4. How do people deal, in their own minds, with these conflicts? Do they:

   a. blame the organization?
   b. blame their supervisors?
   c. blame themselves?
   d. blame their peers?

How do they act as a result of this?

5. Do employees or managers feel that demands are "unfair"? This is often a signal of an organizational demand-worth conflict.

6. Do organizational demands, evaluations, or directives conflict with the employee's sense of a "job well done"? How do employees cope with this in their own minds and in the way they feel and act?

E. Power-Shortage Conflicts

1. Are there positions of power or control without responsibility?

2. Are there responsibilities without power or control?

3. How are the responsibilities evaluated? Can this procedure be changed to reflect the actual power of the person in the position?

4. Can you eliminate
    a. control without responsibility?

    b. responsibility without sufficient control over the situation?

5. Are there worth problems connected to these conflicts or to a solution?

6. How do people cope with the conflicts? How do they have to think of themselves or the job they are doing in order to retain a sense of worth? Who do they blame for their problems with the situation: themselves, others, the organization, or the job?

Job and Status Structure Planning Sheet

Job Task: _____

(for example, "designing high pressure valves")

Employee's Name	Example: Jane Doe										
1. Education	M.A. Engineer										
2. Prior job status	beginning design engineer										
3. Timing in career	2 years experience										
4. Duration in job	9 months										
5. Expectations for Promotion	high expectations										
6. Skill level	moderately experienced engineer										
7. Responsibility	moderate, non-supervisory										
8. Key position in network?	no										
9. Salary	$25,000										
10. Other important statuses	is a woman										

Any place where there is a big difference in status characteristics, e.g., in time in the company or education, you must evaluate whether the difference is likely to become a problem. If there is a problem, it may be solved by acknowledging the difference in some explicit way (e.g., in job title, responsibility, differential pay, or even parking privileges).

167

SUGGESTED READINGS

Readings in Organizational Conflict

Assdel, Henry, "Constructive Role of Interorganizational Conflict," *Administrative Science Quarterly*, 14 (1969), 573-83.

Axelrod, Robert, *Conflict and Interest*. Chicago: Markham, 1970.

Baldridge, J. Victor, *Power and Conflict in the University*. New York: John Wiley and Son, Inc., 1971.

Corwin, Ronald G., "The Professional Employee: A Study of Conflict in Nursing Roles," *American Journal of Sociology*, 66 (1961), 604-15.

Dalton, Melville, "Conflicts between Staff and Line Man Officers," *American Sociological Review*, 15 (1950), 342-51.

Dubin, Robert, "Industrial Conflict: The Power of Prediction," *Industrial and Labor Relations Review*, 18 (1965), 352-63.

Dulton, John M., and Richard E. Walton, "Interdepartmental Conflict and Cooperation: Two Contrasting Studies," *Human Organization*, 25 (1966), 207-20.

Dyer, William G., "Looking at Conflict," *Adult Leadership*, 9 (1960), 79-80.

Evan, William M., "Role Strain and the Norm of Reciprocity in Research Organizations," *American Journal of Sociology*, 68 (1962), 346-54.

Getzels, J.W., and E.G. Guba, "Role, Role Conflict, and Effectiveness," *American Sociological Review*, 19 (1954), 164-75.

Kahn, Robert L., and Elise Boulding (eds.), *Power and Conflict in Organizations*. New York: Basic Books, Inc., 1964.

Kahn, Robert L., Donald M. Wolfe, Robert P. Quinn, J. Diedrick Snaek, and Robert A. Rosenthal, *Organizational Stress: Studies in Role Conflict and Ambiguity*. New York: John Wiley and Son, Inc., 1964.

Katz, Daniel, and Robert L. Kahn, *The Social Psychology of Organizations*. New York: John Wiley and Son, Inc., 1966.

Litwak, Eugene, "Models of Bureaucracy Which Permit Conflict," *American Journal of Sociology*, 67 (1961), 177-84.

Pondy, Louis, "Varieties of Organizational Conflict," *Administration Science Quarterly*, 14 (1969), 499-506.

Rosen, R.A., "Foreman Role Conflict: An Expression of Contradiction in Organizational Goals," *Industrial and Labor Relations Review*, 23 (1970), 541-52.

Rubinton, Earl, "Organizational Strains and Key Roles," *Administrative Science Quarterly*, 9 (1965), 350-69.

Schmidt, Stuart M., and T.A. Kochan, "Conflict: Toward Conceptual Clarity," *Administrative Science Quarterly*, 17 (1972), 359-70.

Simmons, Roberta G., "The Role Conflict of the First-Line Supervisor: An Experimental Study," *American Journal of Sociology*, 73 (1968), 482-95.

Taub, Richard P., *Bureaucracy Under Stress*. Berkeley: University of California Press, 1969.

Thompson, Victor A., "Hierarchy, Specialization, and Organizational Conflict," *Administrative Science Quarterly*, 5 (1961), 485-521.

Walton, Richard E., John W. Dutton, and Thomas P. Cafferty, "Organizational Context and Interdepartmental Conflict," *Administrative Science Quarterly*, 14 (1969), 522-42.

White, Harrison, "Management Conflict and Sociometric Structure," *American Journal of Sociology*, 67 (1966), 185-99.

Readings in Power, Authority, and Structure

Boulding, Kenneth E., *The Organizational Revolution*. New York: Harper & Row, 1953.

Chandler, Alfred D., *Strategy and Structure*. Cambridge, Mass.: The M.I.T. Press, 1962.

Cicourel, Aaron V., "Front and Back of Organizational Leadership: A Case Study," *Pacific Sociological Review*, 1 (1958), 54–58.

Dalton, Gene W., Louis B. Barnes, and Abraham Zaleznik, *The Distribution of Authority in Formal Organizations*. Cambridge, Mass.: The M.I.T. Press, 1973.

Day, Robert, and R.L. Hamblin, "Some Effects of Close and Punitive Styles of Supervision," *American Journal of Sociology*, 69 (1964), 499–510.

Fleishman, Edwin A., and E.F. Harris, "Patterns of Leadership Behavior Related to Employee Grievances and Turnover," *Personnel Psychology*, 15 (1962), 43–56.

Gross, Edward, "Some Functional Consequences of Primary Controls in Formal Work Organization," *American Sociological Review*, 28 (1953), 368–73.

Hollander, E.P., "Style, Structure, and Setting in Organizational Leadership," *Administrative Science Quarterly*, 16 (1971), 1–9.

Jacobs, T.O., *Leadership and Exchange in Formal Organizations*. Alexandria, Va.: Human Resources Research Organization, 1970.

Krupp, Sherman, *Pattern in Organization Analysis*. New York: Holt, Rinehart and Winston, Inc., 1961.

Likert, Rensis, *The Human Organization*. New York: McGraw-Hill Book Company, 1967.

Rose, Jerry D., "The Attribution of Responsibility for Organizational Failure," *Sociology and Social Research*, 53 (1969), 323–32.

Selznick, Philip, *Leadership in Administration*. New York: Harper & Row, 1957.

Tannenbaum, Arnold S., *Control in Organizations*. New York: McGraw-Hill Book Company, 1968.

Tausky, Curt, *Work Organization: Major Theoretical Perspectives*. Itasca, Illinois: F.E. Peacock, 1970.

Thompson, Victor A., *Modern Organization*. New York: Alfred A. Knopf, 1961.

Wyatt, S., "The Study of Work Organization and Supervisory Behavior," *Human Organization*, 23 (1965), 245–53.

Readings in Motivation and Group Process

Argyris, Chris, "The Individual and Organization: Some Problems of Mutual Adjustment," *Administrative Science Quarterly*, 2 (1957), 1–24.

——, "Some Problems in Conceptualizing Organization Climate," *Administrative Science Quarterly*, 2 (1958), 501–52.

Dale, John D., *Wage Incentives and Productivity*. New York: George Elliott, 1958.

Dalton, Melville, "Industrial Controls and Personal Relations," *Social Forces*, 35 (1955), 244–49.

Downs, Anthony, *Inside Bureaucracy*. Boston: Little, Brown and Company, 1967.

Evan, William M., and Roberta G. Simmons, "Organizational Effects of Inequitable Rewards," *Administrative Science Quarterly*, 14 (1969), 224–37.

Herzbert, Frederick, *Work and The Nature of Man*. Cleveland: World Publishing Company, 1966.

Lawrence, P.R., and Joy W. Lorsch, "Differentiation and Integration in Complex Organizations," *Administrative Science Quarterly*, 12 (1967), 1–47.

Levinson, Harry, *The Great Jackass Fallacy*. Boston: Division of Research, Graduate School of Business Administration, Harvard University, 1973.

Miller, George A., and L. Wesley Wager, "Adult Socialization, Organizational Structure and Role Orientation," *Administrative Science Quarterly*, 16 (1971), 151–63.

Roby, Thornton B., *Small Group Performance*. Chicago: Rand McNally, 1968.

Runciman, W.G., *Relative Deprivation and Social Justice*. Berkeley: University of California Press, 1966.

Sayles, Leonard R., *Behavior of Industrial Work Groups*. New York: John Wiley and Son, Inc., 1958.

Turner, Arnold, "What is Feedback?," in *Machines and the Man: A Source Book on Automation*, ed. Robert F. Weeks et al. New York: Appleton-Century-Croft, 1961.

Readings in Organizational Change

Coch, L., and J.R.P. French, "Overcoming Resistance to Change," *Human Relations*, 1 (1948), 512–33.

Ginzbert, E., and W. Reilley, *Effecting Change in Large Organizations*. New York: Columbia University Press, 1966.

Goodaire, D.M., "Changing On-the-Job Behavior: How and Where to Start," *Personnel*, 37 (1960), 58–62.

Hage, Jerald, and Michael Aiken, *Social Change in Complex Organization*. New York: Random House, 1970.

Kaufman, Herbert, *The Limits of Organizational Change*. University, Alabama: The University of Alabama Press, 1971.

Lawrence, Paul R., *The Changing of Organizational Behavior Patterns: A Case Study of Decentralization*. Boston: Harvard University, Graduate School of Business Administration, 1958.

Maniha, John, and Charles Perrow, "Reluctant Organization and the Aggressive Environment," *Administrative Science Quarterly*, 10 (1965), 238–57.

Mann, Floyd C., "Changing Superior-Subordinate Relationships," *Journal of Social Issues*, 7 (1951), 56–63.

Mann, Floyd C., and Lawrence K. Williams, "Some Effects of the Changing Work Environment in the Office," *Journal of Social Issues*, 18 (1962), 90–101.

Thompson, Victor A., *Bureaucracy and Innovation*. University, Alabama: The University of Alabama Press, 1969.

VanderZaden, J.W., "Resistance and Social Change," *Social Forces*, 37 (1959), 312–15.

Readings in New Designs

Argyris, Chris, *The Applicability of Organizational Sociology*. Cambridge: At the University Press, 1972.

Blumberg, Paul, *Industrial Democracy: The Sociology of Participation*. New York: Schocken Books, Inc., 1969.

Burke, W. Warner, and Harvey A. Hornstein, *The Social Technology of Organizational Development*. Fairfax, Virginia: N.T.L. Learning Resources Corp., 1972.

Evan, William M. (ed.), *Organizational Experiments: Laboratory and Field Research*. Harper & Row, 1971.

Hughes, E.C., "Disorganization and Reorganization," *Human Organization*, 21 (1962), 154–61.

Jones, Garth N., "Strategies and Tactics of Planned Organizational Change," *Human Organization*, 24 (1965), 192–200.

Jones, John E., "Re-entry," *The 1975 Annual Handbook for Group Facilitators* (1975), 129–31.

Mott, Paul E., *The Characteristics of Effective Organizations*. New York: Harper & Row, 1972.

Patten, Thomas H., Jr., *Organizational Development Through Team Building*. New York: John Wiley and Son, Inc., 1981.

Rocco, Jr., Carzo, and John N. Yanouzas, "Effects of Flat and Tall Organizational Structures," *Administrative Science Quarterly*, 14 (1969), 179–91.

INDEX